"Women aren't the only ones bombarded with conflicting and harmful messages about their identities. More than ever men face an onslaught of expectations, both from the culture and the church, about what it means to be a 'real man.' Through this treacherous landscape, Carolyn Custis James proves a trustworthy guide. With her characteristic warmth and wisdom, she examines manhood through the lens of Jesus Christ and offers a better way forward for men, a way characterized by partnership, joy, and humility. There are few writers who bring as much clarity and conviction to their work as Carolyn Custis James. This book is biblically faithful, immensely timely, and delightfully readable. Every last page is charged with healing power."

— RACHEL HELD EVANS, author of *A Year of Biblical Womanhood* and *Searching for Sunday*

"*Malestrom* takes a close and provocative look at the dangers of patriarchy by taking a close look at what Scripture says about it. This book will lead you to ponder the type of person God asks all of us—male and female—to be. It is a good question to meditate on."

— DARRELL BOCK, Executive Director of Cultural Engagement and Senior Research Professor of New Testament Studies, Dallas Theological Seminary

"*Malestrom* is not of this world, just like God's kingdom to which it bears witness. Carolyn Custis James is a modern-day Deborah, whose work serves as a prophetic challenge to all men to image Jesus. Against the backdrop of patriarchal and radical feminist perspectives that degrade and discount men, James invites Adam's progeny to display profound courage and dignity as they gain a biblical sense of their true identity. This is not a book for the faint of heart: liberated male readers will join forces with women to conquer despair and celebrate the transformative power of God's cruciform and unifying love."

— PAUL LOUIS METZGER, Professor of Christian Theology & Theology of Culture, Multnomah Biblical Seminary/Multnomah University

"Carolyn Custis James writes with urgency, clarity, and meticulous research about issues that don't just concern every man, but relate to the health and stability of the entire church and our wider world. This is a call for men and women to live in the health and freedom of God's calling for both genders."

— ED CYZEWSKI, author of *A Christian Survival Guide* and *Coffeehouse Theology*

"Finding a crack in the door of patriarchy, which still patterns the life of both the church and the world, Carolyn Custis James swings it wide open, redirecting the gender conversation towards its rightful focus: *the malestrom.* Through careful biblical exegesis and an intersectional awareness of the actual social currents that daily sweep over men and boys, this book rightfully articulates a vision for men rooted in the *imago dei* particularly revealed in the life of Jesus Christ. The church is indebted for this resource for opening up a new set of questions at an accessible level, and for remembering that ultimately what makes something Christian is its ability to conform image of the Son."

— **DREW HART,** writer for *Taking Jesus Seriously,*
a *Christian Century* hosted blog and PhD candidate
at Lutheran Theological Seminary at Philadelphia

"Men have indeed lost sight of who God created them to be as human beings and as men! The signs of this reality are visible all around us. From bloody violence on an international scale to the abuse of the most vulnerable little child in the privacy of a home, from 'fatherless' children to abusive marriages, there just seems to be no end. *Malestrom* does a masterful job of first articulating the catastrophic mess we are in, and then walks the reader through a journey unfolding God's divine vision and plan for man through an engaging study of the men of the Scriptures. I simply could not put this book down. Does it offer a final and definitive solution to the problem that began in Genesis 3? Perhaps not. Has it begun a conversation in my mind? You bet! And this conversation is long overdue within the global church today. A timely, well-articulated, and thought-provoking book!"

— **ABRAHAM GEORGE,** Director of International Church
Mobilization, International Justice Mission

"God's intention for the appropriate flourishing of human life has been severely thwarted by culturally captive expressions of masculinity that have oppressed both women and men. *Malestrom* offers us a reminder from Scripture that God's intention for men was not for a dysfunctional masculinity that devastates the image of God within us. Thank you, Carolyn Custis James, for your historical and theological insights that will reshape how I live out my faith in the world. Thank you for a book that benefits both my son and my daughter."

— **SOONG-CHAN RAH,** Milton B. Engebretson Professor
of Church Growth and Evangelism; author of *Prophetic Lament:*
A Call for Justice in Troubled Times

"Unchristian patterns of culturally conditioned models of masculinity are the norm for many Christian men, with disastrous and, far too often, tragic consequences. By surveying the diverse biblical landscape with wisdom, insight, and conviction, Carolyn Custis James calls for a Christ-centered understanding of 'male,' where men and women are equal image bearers of God, truly one flesh, and thus coworkers in the mission of God on earth. James's *Malestrom* is a prophetic and healing voice."

— PETER ENNS, Abram S. Clemens Professor of Biblical Studies, Eastern University (St. Davids, PA); author of *The Bible Tells Me So: Why Defending Scripture Has Made Us Unable to Read It*

"With wisdom and fresh imagination, *Malestrom* challenges business-as-usual patriarchy and calls men and women of faith to a deeper and richer Blessed Alliance. In this inviting and absorbing book, Carolyn Custis James probes the narrative of Holy Scripture and concludes that patriarchy is 'in, but not of' the Bible. As I read, I began to envision what masculinity might mean when redefined from a kingdom perspective that inverts the social pyramid that so distorts our gendered lives. With more in mind than just a kinder and gentler patriarchy, James opens up the Scriptures, directing the reader through the pitfalls of traditional thinking about men, women, power, and hierarchy. As you turn pages you'll meet anew people like Abraham, Judah, Barak, Boaz, Matthew, Joseph, and pivotal women of the Bible who, through God's grace, come to stand against the malestrom and enter into the new hope of Jesus of Nazareth. A bracing book for an embattled world; I read hungrily and came away nourished."

— MATTHEW S. VOS, Covenant College, Department of Sociology

"In *Malestrom*, Carolyn Custis James takes us by the hand and leads us through the story of how God dismantles patriarchy in the Bible. By the time we're done reading, a new space has been cleared. Men can now be men. Women can now be women. And together we can live God's gendered salvation. It is a remarkable accomplishment."

— DAVID FITCH, B. R. Lindner Chair of Evangelical Theology, Northern Seminary

"This is the book I've been waiting for—as a wife, as a mother of a son, as a woman committed to the blessed alliance God intended between men and women. This book will be healing and restorative for so many. It's a beautiful invitation to manhood in the Kingdom of God."

— SARAH BESSEY, author of *Jesus Feminist* and *Out of Sorts*

malestrom

MANHOOD SWEPT INTO THE CURRENTS OF
A CHANGING WORLD

CAROLYN CUSTIS JAMES

ZONDERVAN

Malestrom
Copyright © 2015 by Carolyn Custis James

This title is also available as a Zondervan ebook. Visit www.zondervan.com/ebooks.

This title is also available in a Zondervan audio edition. Visit www.zondervan.fm.

Requests for information should be addressed to:

Zondervan, 3900 *Sparks Dr. SE, Grand Rapids, Michigan 49546*

Library of Congress Cataloging-in-Publication Data

James, Carolyn Custis, 1948 – author.
    Malestrom : manhood swept into the currents of a changing world / Carolyn
Custis James.
       pages   cm
       ISBN 978-0-310-32557-4 (hardback)
       1. Christian men – Religious life. I. Title.
    BV4528.2.J355 2015
    248.8′42 – dc23   2014049414

15 16 17 18 19 20 21 22 23 24 25 /DCI/ 20 19 18 17 16 15 14 13 12 11 10 9 8 7 6 5 4 3 2 1

In loving memory of—

my father

L Dwight Custis
(1920—2012)
who taught me to love the Scriptures
and to keep digging to learn more.
I miss him every day.

my brother-in-law

Jeffrey Kelly James
(1958—2006)
who lit up every room he entered
and
never saw a mountain he didn't want to climb.

my namesake

Solomon James Jeffrey Rossi-Keen
(2014)
who never saw the light of day.
"Solomon" because his father wanted him to be wise
and
"James" because his mother wanted him
to be a warrior for Jesus.

CONTENTS

FOREWORD

Consider this foreword a postcard from the malestrom. As one born and bred in the malestrom, I know what it feeds on and how it breeds. I know from firsthand experience the father wound (see Carolyn's chapter on this) that burdens so many males. Without good role models, we flounder as young men and sometimes embrace a cultural vision of manhood that bears little resemblance to Jesus. I also know from my own life experiences that even as men pursue the various culturally defined visions of manhood, it is often accompanied by a gnawing sense within us (the *imago dei*) that there is something not quite right about our behaviors and attitudes—the constant jousting for superiority, the artificial machismo, the domineering bravado, the denigration of the weaker males, and the sexualizing of women that shapes so much of male conversation.

The truth is that the malestrom produces schizophrenic males. We present to the world one version of ourselves for external consumption. We hide the true self with its wounds and vulnerabilities. Sometimes we bury the authentic self so deeply that it surfaces only when lubricated by alcohol or drugs. This schizophrenic maleness proliferates in our homes, locker rooms, movie theaters, magazines, blogs, and to our shame, our pulpits, Sunday school classes, and campus ministries. And yes, it is alive and well in our evangelical seminaries.

As a historian, I have taken a sacred vow to tell the truth even when it is painful. A few days from now I will lecture on *church* history and, although it grieves me to say it, far too much of our history is fraught with male aggression against various opponents—often fellow Christians. I will have to tell the story of the brutality of the crusades, the pogroms against the Jews, the Salem witch trials, the wars of religion, the marginalization of our sisters, the advocacy of slavery, and the internal power struggles that scar our story. If I am honest, I must confess that men have taken the lead role in this history of the church. Admittedly, this is not a comfortable story to tell, nor is it pleasant to see the face of a student at the moment of awful recognition that this is *our* story.

It might be argued that, in a broad sense, church history is essentially the struggle of what it means to be a Christian man. To be sure, most Christian men do not express their manhood through acts of physical violence, but that is not to say there is not an intense internal conflict between their Christian ideals and the cultural conceptions of manhood.

The fall of Adam is worse than we imagined. Theologians are skilled at giving abstract and dispassionate theological analyses of the fall. Carolyn's book reminds us that the malestrom and its impact on males is never a mere abstraction. The malestrom is the ugly consequence of the fall for the male species.

Over the years, I have had the privilege of reading drafts of Carolyn's books, and inevitably there are poignant moments that bring me to tears. Not so with this book. The overwhelming emotion in reading this book was a mixture of sadness and apprehension. My sadness is that the life and teaching of Jesus seem to have been missed for so long. Part of the power of the malestrom is that it obscures our reading of the biblical text and so our pulpits promulgate unhealthy notions of manhood.

My apprehension is derived from the anxiety that escape from this cultural captivity of manhood will not come easily. Jesus' own disciples demonstrate the difficulty. Blinded by the malestrom, they failed to grasp that Rabbi Jesus was inaugurating a new kingdom—not of this world. It was not a kingdom that engages in violence to overthrow the brutish Roman government nor was it a hierarchical kingdom of superiors and inferiors. It was a kingdom of grace, mercy, and humility. This new kingdom of Jesus is comprised of those who turn the other cheek and where the last is first. This new kingdom is to be populated with a new kind of male, the kind of male who comes to life in Carolyn's book. These men resist the malestrom and give us a new vision of manhood for this new kingdom. My sadness and apprehension remain, but they are tempered by hope and the transforming power of the Holy Spirit.

I confess that I have a vested interest in seeing Carolyn's book read widely by both women and men. She is an insightful guide to steer us through our cultural blind spots to see what has been there all the time: a Bible that rejects patriarchy for the distortion that it is. I can speak with some authority about Carolyn's extraordinary insight because I have been its first beneficiary.

FRANK A. JAMES III

PRESIDENT AND PROFESSOR OF HISTORICAL THEOLOGY

BIBLICAL THEOLOGICAL SEMINARY

Acknowledgments

THIS BOOK HAS BEEN SIMMERING on a back burner for several years. The title of the book I wrote before this one, *Half the Church*, signaled an incompleteness to the discussion of God's vision for his image bearers that needed to be addressed. The stories of men who appeared alongside the stories of women featured in my earlier books kept pointing me in this direction.

I've never found writing books to come easy. But I never imagined the miracle it would take to finish this one. As a woman, writing a book about men naturally took me out of my comfort zone. The timing of this particular book was complicated even further by coinciding with one of the most stressful stretches of my life. God has been merciful to me in so many ways.

The idea of the book was birthed in Florida. The project took shape in Massachusetts as I researched what is happening with men and boys globally. The actual writing took place in Pennsylvania at various locations—a basement apartment (a.k.a. the "Hobbit Hole"), a vacant office in the upper regions of Biblical Theological Seminary, and the final touches in my home office where I am surrounded by unpacked moving boxes.

Forward progress was repeatedly hindered by, among other things, the critical illness and death of my beloved father, two major moves, and eight miserable months of separation from Frank when his new job as President at BTS took him to Philadelphia and our Boxford, Massachusetts house stubbornly refused to sell. That delay involved coping solo with one of the worst winters in recent New England history—fun things like

13

shoveling snow over and over again, a wreck with my car, and trouble with the heating system. Just as movers were loading our belongings into the van, I was diagnosed with cancer. Major surgery followed in Philly, from which I am still recovering. On the bright side, Frank and I traveled to Florida one month after my surgery in time for the birth of our beautiful granddaughter, Arden Olivia.

It has been a battle to the very last paragraph, and I am overwhelmed with gratitude to those who pulled and pushed and prayed me over the finish line. Every single word of encouragement made a difference.

I'm especially grateful:

For my husband, Frank, who never doubted the importance of this project and believed in me every step of the way. What a gift you are. Thanks for all those grocery runs and fast-food meals. Chick-fil-A loves you and so do I! Above all, thanks for the rich conversations and editing. I could not have done this without you.

For my daughter Allison, whose "You can do it!" text messages and frequent pictures of Arden cheered me on again and again. Thank God for the blessings of technology and for a daughter who knows how to use it and loves to keep in touch with her mom!

For my faithful band of praying friends—Susan Green, Lori Lambelet, Susan Nash, Linda Parkhouse, Brooke Sulahian, Karen Wilson, and Cathey and Mark Anderson. There are others, I know. It made a world of difference to know you were all praying for me.

For my friends at Zondervan, who have blessed me with their steadfast support and patience and whose enthusiasm for this project has never faltered despite the delays: Stan Gundry, who has supported me with wise counsel and friendship from my first book proposal. I know plenty of other authors will agree with me that Katya Covrett is the best editor anyone could have.

What a great friend she has become. This is the third book that Verlyn Verbrugge has edited. I love working with him, and he always makes my books better. His commitment to see this book through to publication in the midst of his own battle with cancer is a gift I will never forget. Verlyn Verbrugge's thoughtful editing always makes my writing better. It's a gift to have Jesse Hillman's creative marketing advocacy behind my writing efforts and my words wrapped in Rob Monacelli's artistic jacket design. And Kait Lamphere has done an amazing job on the interior design of the book.

For Erik Wolgemuth, who looks out for me in so many ways and has been incredibly supportive and encouraging through this entire project.

For Amy Lauger for helping me with statistics, and for Old Testament scholar David Lamb for interacting with my ideas.

Now as I savor the relief that comes with finishing and you, the reader, take up this book and begin to read, my prayer is that you will become as troubled as I am over the crisis of identity and purpose facing men and boys globally that I have dubbed *the malestrom*. My hope is that, as you read, your hope in Jesus and his gospel will be renewed. May you be fortified to resist the malestrom's powerful currents and may you delight in the greater countercultural power of the kingdom of Jesus. Above all, may the men in your life find deep resonance with the incredible rediscovered men whose stories are in this book.

THE MALESTROM

The maelstrom is the seaman's nightmare, but the "malestrom" poses an even greater threat to men than the hidden dangers of the open seas.

MAELSTROMS—THOSE POWERFUL SWIRLING whirlpools in the open seas—have been known to pull hapless fishing boats, crew, and cargo down into a deadly vortex to the ocean's dark depths. Maelstroms take on epic proportions in the world of fiction. In Edgar Allan Poe's short story, "A Descent into the Maelstrom," the lone survivor of a maelstrom recounts the harrowing tale of how he and his two brothers sailed once too often into dangerous but lucrative fishing waters and were swept into the jaws of Moskstraumen, a large maelstrom off the Norwegian coast. Overnight the trauma of his terrifying ordeal turned the storyteller into an old man, or so it seemed. "You suppose me a *very* old man, but I am not. It took less than a single day to change these hairs from a jetty black to white, to weaken my limbs, and to unstring my nerves."[1]

If the vivid image of the maelstrom seems frightening and destructive, its powers pale in comparison to the damaging currents and global reach of the *male*strom. While the maelstrom that Poe's hero encountered poses a threat to sailors and fishermen taking occasional careless risks at sea, the malestrom's reach is global and relentless. It isn't overstating things to say there isn't a man or boy alive who isn't a target. The malestrom's global currents can be violent and overt, but also come in subtle, even benign forms that catch men unawares. *The malestrom is the particular ways in which the fall impacts the male of the human species—causing a man to lose himself, his identity and purpose as a man, and above all to lose sight of God's original vision for his sons.* The repercussions of such devastating personal losses are not merely disastrous for the men themselves, but catastrophic globally.

Issues raised by the malestrom go well beyond the localized, insular evangelical gender debates over manhood and womanhood that have become the central focus of the western church when it comes to talking about men. A discussion of rules and roles and of who gets to lead and who doesn't, laments over alleged "feminization," Father's Day tongue-lashings from the pulpit, and the need to "Man up!" grossly underestimate and actually fail to recognize the greater real and more pressing issues facing men. Issues regarding men that occupy the evangelical church also trivialize and become a distraction from the rich potential God has entrusted to his sons. Instead, the malestrom actually feeds on this misfocus and gains momentum when the church turns inward and offers so-called "manly" solutions that only work for some men and even then can prove unsustainable in something as commonplace as a job layoff, a medical crisis, a divorce, or the realities of old age.

The malestrom is one of the Enemy's single most ingenious and successful strategies. Its victories are flashed before us every day in the headlines as men lose sight of who God created them to be as men.

MALESTROM, MASCULINITY, AND VIOLENCE

As I write, the media is ablaze with reports of appalling levels of violence around the world. The Middle East is a cauldron of warfare with Hamas and Israel acting on the ancient Near

Eastern ethic of *lex talionis* (eye-for-an-eye retaliation) with rocket fire and guided missiles. City after city in Iraq has fallen to the relentless march of ISIS militants, accompanied by savage executions of Iraqi citizens—not only Shia Muslims, but also Christians, Yazidis, and other religious minorities—that shock the sensibilities of the civilized world. The Ukraine is embroiled in a bloody civil war with rebels fueled by Russian military support. Here at home, US cities are smoldering with racial unrest and angry protests after police shot and killed an unarmed black male youth in Ferguson, Missouri. Another school shooting (accompanied by the young male gunman's suicide) devastates and forever alters a quiet suburban community. By the time this book rolls off the presses, new calamities will be dominating the news.

These tragic events have one thing in common: *male violence.* (Yes, women are involved in this bloodshed, but they represent a tiny fraction of this insanity.) Dare I say it? This is the history of the planet in microcosm—men killing others. In the beginning, the first sin after the fall was Cain's killing of Abel.

Lest we underestimate the connection between the malestrom and male violence, perhaps we should consider the comments of anthropologist David Gilmore who explicitly linked "masculine pride" to violent conflicts in the world. He asserts that such violence is "as much a product of a manhood image as ... political and economic demands."[2] Sociologists are all too aware that there is an insidious link between masculinity and violence that fuels many of the wars that rage across our world.[3]

The need to establish and maintain one's manhood drives men into violent actions and exerts constant pressure for men to prove themselves. It fuels aggression, competition, and self-interest, and creates countless casualties at the giving and receiving ends of violence and injustice. It feeds the illusion that behind every change in the culture, every alteration in circumstances, lurks a threat to one's right to call himself a man.

Malestrom violence is often directed toward other men. They are humiliated and stripped of dignity as human beings and demeaned as men by the downward currents of injustice, systemic poverty, racism, classism, homophobia, xenophobia, bullying, and a plethora of other abuses inflicted largely by other men. A staggering 30 percent of those who are trafficked globally for forced labor or sex are men and boys—a number that roughly approximates the entire population of New York City proper.[4] In wars, countless men are slaughtered, permanently disabled, or left suffering with post-traumatic stress disorder (PTSD)—scarred by what they've witnessed, suffered, or inflicted on others. PTSD is not just a military issue; it plagues young men living in our inner cities. At the Center for Disease Control, it was noted "that children who live in inner cities experience higher rates of PTSD than do combat veterans, due in large part to the fact that the majority of kids living in inner city neighborhoods are routinely exposed to violence."[5]

What has until recently gone unnoticed is how the malestrom touches down in the lives of men and boys who on the surface (and even as far as they can tell) seem to escape all this violence but who are nonetheless also victims. They become emotional islands—unable to acknowledge, much less express their feelings. Through cultural conditioning that takes both benign and violent forms, they are cut off from significant God-given parts of themselves that lead to human wholeness for fear it will make them less of a man. There's a social price to be paid for the boy who mistakenly manifests some culturally defined "unmanly" trait. A boy can be disqualified by a lack of interest in hunting, fishing, sports, cage-fighting, and other so-called "wild-man activities," or if his natural gifts fall at the other end of the spectrum—arts, poetry, literature, for example. The social price this exacts can be devastating. Stephen Boyd reminds us:

> We men are not inherently or irreversibly violent, relationally incompetent, emotionally constipated, and sexually

compulsive. To the extent that we manifest these characteristics, we do so not because we are male, but because we have experienced violent socialization and conditioning processes that have required or produced this kind of behavior and we have chosen to accept, or adopt, these ways of being, thinking, and acting.[6]

While there are lots of contributing factors to all these forms of violence, one explanation goes right to the heart of what this book is all about: *Men have lost sight of who God created them to be as human beings and as men.*

This is the malestrom's ultimate triumph. It is a crisis of catastrophic proportions. Questions about the malestrom and manhood are not localized western church issues. They are global, cultural, and timeless issues. It is not possible to engage the malestrom adequately if we persist in developing our theology of male and female cloistered within the controlled environment of a prosperous, privileged, white, middle-class, heterosexual, suburban demographic. We won't ask the right questions and we can't count on our answers if we only have this narrow subgroup in mind. To paraphrase for men what I wrote for women,

a global conversation safeguards us from proclaiming a prosperity gospel for [men] that works for some (at least for a time) and is utterly crushing to vast numbers of [men] in our own culture and elsewhere in the world.... Global thinking raises deeper questions and sends us in search of answers that are expansive and dynamic enough to frame every [man's] life from birth to death. Within this wider global context, we will discover the true strength of God's message for [men].... This is where we will plumb the depths of God's love for his [sons] and see for ourselves that no life is ever beyond the reach of the gospel's restorative powers, no matter how a [man's] story plays out. Until we go global, we can never be sure of our questions, much less the answers we affirm.[7]

Widening this discussion to the global level not only gives us greater respect for the complexities that men and boys are facing, it also means we cannot get away with simplistic solutions men everywhere can't count on and that are ultimately hurtful.

THE MANHOOD MATRIX

One of the pressing issues lurking behind male violence is the persistent question of manhood. Theologians and social scientists generally agree that sex and gender are *not* the same. *Sex* refers to biology—to *physical differences* in anatomy that distinguish males from females. *Gender* refers to how a particular culture defines *what it means* to be male (manhood/masculinity) or *what it means* to be female (womanhood/femininity).

From a sociological perspective, manhood is a cultural construct or a human invention.[8] Social historian E. Anthony Rotundo observes that "each culture constructs its own version of what men ... are—and ought to be."[9] Because manhood is a cultural construct, the definition of manhood is not universal but varies widely from culture to culture. In fact, in some cultures (including our own) multiple definitions of manhood are operative at the same time. Sometimes, an individual man is simultaneously juggling more than one definition himself if he inhabits more than one culture or subculture.

Anthropologists describe a *continuum of manhood* that ranges from *machismo* (a strong, aggressive, masculine pride and bravado) at one extreme to cultures completely unconcerned about masculinity issues at the other. Modern urban western versions of manhood land somewhere in the middle.[10] Evangelical definitions of manhood—all claiming to be built on what the Bible says—are scattered all over that continuum.

Three core responsibilities for men are found in a majority of manhood definitions: to father children, to protect the family, and to provide for their sustenance. Gilmore calls this "Man the Impregnator-Protector-Provider."[11]

In cultures where physical survival is a daily challenge, manhood is a life-and-death issue. If a nearby hostile tribe or state threatens to cross boundary lines and wage an assault, the whole community is endangered if men refuse to defend them. Likewise, starvation is a real threat if men fail to fulfill their hunting role. Nor can at-risk cultures afford for young men to fritter away their adulthood and not get busy producing children, especially where there are high rates of infant mortality. The future of any culture is jeopardized without a thriving next generation.

If things weren't complicated enough, manhood is also *a moving target* that shifts in response to cultural changes and developments. American culture is a classic example. Since the start of our country's brief history, in response to cultural and economic changes, manhood has morphed from simply heading the family, to a man's occupation,[12] to being defined "by money and aggression, by posture and swagger and 'props,' by the curled lip and petulant sulk and flexed biceps, by the glamour of the cover boy, and by the market-bartered 'individuality' that sets one astronaut or athlete or gangster above another."[13]

Today's globalized Internet-connected world continues to impact how men see themselves and makes change inevitable. Social media connects the world in new and helpful ways — which inevitably brings greater access to information and ideas. Every day, round the clock, we are bombarded with a constant barrage of global news that opens our eyes to real-time information and innovations beyond the imagination of previous generations.

The Internet has created a virtual parallel universe where instantaneous communication, access to information, and unfettered freedom of speech have exploded. Voices that formerly were silenced have set up camp in the blogosphere and are fearlessly challenging the status quo on formerly taboo subjects such as gender, sexuality, racism, all forms of abuse, and a host of other justice issues. Yet, even amid these massive cultural shifts, the changing landscape hasn't come with changed attitudes about masculinity. Sociologist Michael Kimmel asserts that while "the world has changed dramatically ... most men still cling tenaciously to an ideology of masculinity that comes off the set of *Mad Men*."[14]

In addition to Gilmore's man as impregnator-protector-provider, perhaps the most enduring distinctive of manhood definitions is *the polarization of men and women*. The one thing most men are quick to assert is that he is *"not a woman."* In many cultures, one of the first essential steps toward manhood is separating young boys from their mothers to avoid excessive female influence. Yet many men—notably professional athletes raised by single mothers—openly acknowledge their mother's primary influence in making men out of them.

The scorning of all things feminine and the establishment of "separate spheres" (supposedly brought on by the Industrial Revolution but actually much older than that) underscores the need for manhood to be distinct from anything female—a trend with costly side effects for both men and women. It reinforces and perpetuates a division that was never meant to be and that cuts both off from God-given strengths they were created to give and need from one another. It also pressures men to deny and repress the deep sensitivities they actually feel for fear of appearing weak or being ridiculed for acting "like a girl."

The Rite to Manhood

Regardless of how a culture may define manhood, "real" manhood is *not a birthright*. It must be earned. Generally speaking, many cultures assume a girl arrives at womanhood when her body matures. But for a boy to become a man and do what his community needs to survive, he has to be motivated. Real manhood "is a precarious or artificial state that boys must win against powerful odds."[15]

Many cultures employ formal initiation rites to transition boys into men. In some cultures, these rites take brutal forms physically, psychologically, and socially. Boys are subjected to and must willingly endure (without wincing or crying out) what westerners would classify as physical torture and human rights violations: violent beatings, cuttings, and burnings with hot coals that leave permanent "manly" scars. Some carry out sexual rites too graphic and abusive to describe. The justification for such violent passages to manhood is that survival depends on men tackling dangerous, unpleasant, or laborious tasks. Boys must be motivated to man up.[16]

Formal initiation rites may not exist in the West, but that doesn't mean conformity to so-called "masculine" standards won't be enforced through peer-pressure, bullying, and locker-room violence. Even in the evangelical church, manhood must be earned and dangles from a slender thread of a man's ability to bring home the bacon and to assume spiritual leadership over his wife. Men frequently hear the thunderous epithet from Christian pulpits: "You are not a real man if ..." followed by some arbitrary masculine requirement that for all sorts of reasons, some men are not able or don't need to fulfill. One pastor spelled out five milestones to manhood: leave your parents' home, get an education, land a "real" job, marry a wife, and father children. How many men does that road map exclude?

Manhood can be flunked, denied, missed, or withdrawn.

WOMEN AND THE MALESTROM

Both men and women are caught up in the malestrom. One cannot speak of males without taking females into consideration. The two are inseparable. Indeed, many of the same issues that emerged in my study of women have resurfaced in my research of men. As I have reflected on this, it should not be surprising. Are not both men and women striving to make their way in a messy fallen world where it is easy to forget who God created us to be? Indeed, writing about women is what convinced me to take up the subject of men. God's purposes for his daughters are not ends in themselves, but are fundamentally connected to and essential to God's purposes for his sons. Men *belong* in the discussion about women—not as observers or merely "to understand women better" (which I've been told wouldn't interest some men anyway), but as *participants* with a vested interest in the conversation and without whom the conversation is incomplete.

The full flourishing of God's sons requires and even depends on the full flourishing of his daughters. It works both ways. No matter how much ground we've covered in the discussion of the Bible's message for women, until we join that discussion with an equally robust discussion of men, significant pieces are missing and we're left hanging.

Gender debate fatigue is spreading in the church. For too long, our discussions of gender have tilted to one side or the other, sometimes reaching toxic levels and accompanied by a pendulum swinging logic that leads us to believe advocacy for one gender comes at a cost for the other. No resolution is in sight. There's a sense that we're somehow stuck in a zero-sum game, sparring like bickering siblings over a finite pie, each vying to get their fair share. Or we regard discussions of God's purposes for his sons and daughters as separate and unrelated issues unless, of course, one side seems to encroach on territory belonging to the other.

The Bible doesn't present different or competing visions for God's sons and daughters. God's vision for his world is singular, whole, and unified. Male and female callings are not separate issues. They are interwoven, interdependent, and inseparable in the Bible. God didn't create a world where one gender can flourish at the expense of the other. In God's world, the true flourishing of one *depends* on and *promotes* the full flourishing of the other. In fact, God's kingdom purposes for the world hinge on how well we *both* flourish and pull together to serve him.

Contrary to that vision, women are perceived as one of the greatest threats to manhood. Probably no cultural change has reconfigured the social landscape or unsettled men more than the rise of women. The Women's Movement is one of the biggest cultural shifts of the last fifty years. Following the publication of Betty Friedan's *Feminine Mystique* and the launch of Second Wave Feminism in the 1960s, women broke through glass ceilings in every field and profession and secured a place at "the table" both in secular and religious contexts. The "New Girl Order" was breaking up the "Old Boys' Club"—upending traditional assumptions, dislodging men from places they previously owned by default, and raising widespread concerns among men.

Feminism has gone global with an all-out effort to achieve human rights for women and girls everywhere, and there will be no turning back. The New Girl Order is in many ways a good thing as advocacy for women and girls expands and they are valued, educated, and empowered to flourish and contribute to their communities in countless ways. But the impact on men and boys can result in a loss of self and place. Many men welcome the changes, are staunch advocates for women, and value the contributions women are making. And yet, progress for women has changed the terrain significantly and means changes for them too. Men must now compete with women for positions a man previously held by default.

As women gain financial independence and self-confidence, the traditional male role as provider and protector is eroding. Women can protect and provide for themselves. Thanks to sperm donors, some single women (known as "choice-mothers") have gone so far as to make babies without a man and raise children on their own.[17]

It is a new world with unexpected developments and changes rippling out in all directions. Boys are underperforming in school. Women are outdistancing men in numbers as college and graduate school students and have careers (not domesticity) on their minds. In Christian circles we may debate forever over who leads in church and in the home. But the debate is over when a man sets foot outside the door on Monday and heads into the workplace where his boss could easily be a woman.

In response, masculinity movements, men's rights organizations, man-events, and retreats to teach boys to hunt and fish and do other manly activities have surfaced here and there. None have had the kind of sustained momentum or widespread support that the women's movement achieved. Frequent protests are heard from men both outside and inside the church that they are losing previously all-male turf due to "feminism" and "feminization." But when men still hold the reins of power, it's difficult to blame women for changes they are weathering.

Economic changes are also giving women a new advantage over men. Along with the 2008 economic crisis that put a lot of men out of work, the shift from an industrial to a knowledge-based economy brought new opportunities that are generally better suited to women's skills and acumen.

> In the past men derived their advantage largely from size and strength, but the postindustrial economy is indifferent to brawn. A service and information economy rewards precisely the opposite qualities—the ones that can't be easily replaced by a machine. These attributes—social intelligence, open communication, the ability to sit still and focus—are, at a minimum, not predominantly the province of men. In fact, they seem to come more easily to women.[18]

The combination of the rise of women and this economic shift has profoundly impacted growing numbers of affluent, western, predominantly white young men. They are increasingly adrift without a life script or the default male privileges that formerly gave them solid footing. They are missing clear milestones in their transition from adolescence into adulthood. Forward progress has stalled for enough of them to warrant creation of a new demographic described as "prolonged male adolescence" or SYMs— Single Young Men—the label marketers gave them. SYMs may go straight from college to a high-paying job, but marriage, mortgage payments, and parenthood? They're in no rush and don't see marriage or fatherhood as required rites of manhood.

Success in this economy requires more education. College loans take the appeal out of adding the financial obligations of a wife, a home mortgage, and kids. The pill and sexual freedoms won by the Women's Movement have made premarital sex more readily available and removed the stigma for women of previous generations and other patriarchal cultures. She'll even buy dinner. SYMs are often characterized by plenty of pocket money and obsessions with video games, partying, hook-ups, and general bad-boy behavior modeled after the media's comedic portrayals of guys stuck in this demographic.

Disturbing as some of these developments are, they are merely symptoms that divert our attention from the core problem that has caused men to veer off-course from who God created them to be. Deciding which cultural definition of manhood is right or finally declaring a winner in the church's gender debate stops short of real global solutions or of taking seriously the profoundly human questions that are at stake. The malestrom is a much deeper systemic issue the consequences of which are (even in its mildest forms) a destructive distortion and loss of what it means to be a man or boy designed to reflect the Creator.

There may not be a universal cultural definition of manhood. But the issues that drive the quest for manhood are universal— a fundamental quest for identity, meaning, and purpose. The global nature of the issues was never more starkly demonstrated than when experts began analyzing what to do about ISIS and why so many young men (including some from the United States and Europe) are being drawn to this violent movement. John

L. Esposito (Professor of Religion and International Affairs, Georgetown University) makes the case that men are drawn to ISIS in search of *"a new identity, and for a sense of meaning, purpose and belonging."*[19] Huffington Post Executive Religion Editor, Rev. Paul Brandeis Raushenbush, echoed that conclusion when he observed that a key factor is *"a lack of meaning and purpose in life."*[20]

PATRIARCHY AND THE MALESTROM

Trace any current of the malestrom to its roots, and you'll end up looking at patriarchy ("father rule"). The prevalent features of manhood definitions are man as impregnator, protector, provider, and polar opposite of women. These are distinct characteristics of the patriarchal social system. Questions that ultimately confront every man and boy and drive his choices center on the quest for identity, meaning, purpose, and belonging. These are questions patriarchy proposes to answer.

The malestrom can be conceived from several different angles. All forms of patriarchy are not equally bad—patriarchy is a continuum. It ranges from radicalized violent fundamentalists, such as the Taliban and ISIS (but that exist in every religion, including Christianity), to kinder, gentler versions embraced and promoted by cultural traditionalists and some western evangelicals. Despite the vast variety of expressions, the root issues of the malestrom run deeper than gender; they are about what Jesus warned us—of the original sin of self-interest, privilege, dominance, and power over others.

This book argues that *the principal expression of the malestrom is historic patriarchy.* Further, I'm convinced that patriarchy, while alluring to many, is ultimately destructive for both men and women. But above all, it runs counter to the gospel of Jesus. Jesus didn't come to make men more manly, but to reconnect them with their Creator and put them back on mission as God's image bearers. Patriarchy remains a powerful force in today's world. Defined broadly,

> patriarchy is a social system in which the role of the male as the primary authority figure is central to social organization, and where fathers hold authority over women, children, and property. It implies the institutions of male rule and privilege, and is dependent on female subordination. Historically, the principle of patriarchy has been central to the social, legal, political, and economic organization of Hebrew, Greek, Roman, Indian, and Chinese cultures, and has had a deep influence on modern civilization.[21]

If men must rule—whether in government, on the streets, or in private homes—then anything that threatens a man's place of authority also jeopardizes his manhood.

For Christians the prominence of patriarchy on the pages of the Bible means patriarchy is important for a variety of reasons, regardless of what our personal views may be of that cultural system. First, patriarchy matters because it is the cultural backdrop of the Bible. Beginning with Abraham, God chose patriarchs living in a patriarchal culture to launch his rescue effort for the world. Events in the Bible play out within a patriarchal context. But patriarchy is not the Bible's message. Rather, it is the fallen cultural backdrop that sets off in the strongest relief the radical nature and potency of the Bible's gospel message. We need to understand that world and patriarchy in particular—much better than we do—if we hope to grasp the radical countercultural message of the Bible.

Second, patriarchy matters because the prevalence of this cultural system on the pages of Scripture, in cultures around the world, and throughout history can easily lead (and has led) to the assumption that patriarchy is divinely ordained. Many believe this is the way God wants us to live, even though westerners who embrace patriarchy are selective about the few patriarchal elements they retain from the Bible—which is itself an admission that something may be wrong with the system. Most throw out slavery and polygamy, along with associating disappointment and failure with the birth of a daughter, child brides, honor killings, and inheritance laws, for example. But they cling fervently to male leadership and female submission in the home and in the church. Some extend these male/female dynamics to include the wider culture.

In a determination to defend patriarchy against the tide of social changes in western society, some patriarchalists claim to detect "whispers of male headship" in the creation narrative (Genesis 1–2), even though patriarchy doesn't surface until *after* the fall when the curse that men will rule women is felt and the prospect of men ruling over other men (which is also inherent in patriarchy) surfaces too. Before the fall, the Bible goes on record with some pretty straightforward antipatriarchal statements. Still other patriarchal advocates go so far as to elevate patriarchy to a level equal to the gospel and to question the orthodoxy and commitment to the Bible's authority of fellow Christians who don't share their perspective.[22]

The danger is that a basic belief in the essential goodness of patriarchy can cordon off the topic from honest discussion. It can prevent us from asking some of the hard, uncomfortable questions that the Bible invites or from examining honestly the negative effects of this cultural system within biblical times, as well as today.

Here's the problem: so long as patriarchy is enthroned as the gender message of the Bible, it poses a significant barrier to a strong and flourishing Blessed Alliance[23] between men and women and a healthy, fully functioning body of Christ, which in turn inevitably hinders God's mission in the world. It gives us no alternative but to circle the wagons theologically to protect this system, rather than the freedom to engage the cultural shifts and changes happening all around us. The kinder-gentler nuanced version of patriarchy often preached from Christian pulpits merely situates Christians on the world's patriarchal continuum and by blending in (even as a much improved version) renders the church incapable of generating jaw-dropping evidence that Jesus has come and that his kingdom is "not of this world."[24]

CONFRONTING THE MALESTROM

The malestrom poses one of the most serious historic challenges to the gospel. Does the gospel have anything better to offer men than a kinder, gentler patriarchy? Is the gospel able to fill the manhood void with an indestructible identity and calling that cover the entire cultural spectrum and the complete lifespan of a man's life—no matter how long or how short that may be or how his story plays out? This is not simply an internal church issue. We have ISIS to consider. Men in today's world are looking for answers.

I would never have attempted a book like this if I weren't convinced the malestrom is no match for the gospel of Jesus Christ. I do not say this lightly or as some religious pat answer to the problems I have seen. If anything, my research has made me as concerned about the plight of men as I have ever been about women and girls. Nor am I suggesting that the malestrom is easily managed. The malestrom belongs to life in a fallen world. It will be with us wreaking havoc until Jesus comes. What it does mean, and I say this with conviction, is that as Christians we have been empowered by God's Spirit to engage this battle for men and boys, to dismantle false and destructive manhood definitions, and reclaim radically redemptive ways of being human that God envisioned for his sons in the beginning.

Having said that, two major problems confront us before we even begin: first, that a chapter is missing from the Bible that is most pertinent to our quest, and second, that the men in the Bible best equipped to help us have gone missing too.

The missing chapter comes between creation and the fall. The Bible's two opening chapters begin with the hopeful expansive vision God is casting for the world he created and loves and where he designates his male and female image bearers together to get the job done. But before we witness a single moment of unfallen image bearer living or see how male and female align to reflect God's image and engage his mission in the world—an enemy invades. God's image bearers rebel, and we are left in the ruins of a fallen world searching for clues to tell us what he had in mind for us. It's like trying to assemble a Mercedes from broken, rusted auto parts salvaged from a junkyard when you've never seen a Mercedes.

We need that missing chapter.

This omission is not a mistake or a publishing snafu, but an Authorial decision intended to make us dissatisfied and hungry for something more and better than anything we've yet seen. It makes us hungry for Jesus, who is the missing chapter and embodies the kind of image bearer God created all of his sons (and daughters) to become. Jesus didn't come just to tweak things, but to overthrow the kingdom of this world. We are slow to learn and need more stories to help us catch God's kingdom vision and even to help us make sense of the example Jesus sets for us.

This is where the missing men come in.

Interwoven in the stories of women in the Bible that I have developed in my previous books[25] are men whose stories are eclipsed by a larger personality who commands the spotlight or men whose stories are diminished, downsized, or distorted because we view them through a western lens. We gravitate instead to men like Joseph, who rises from slavery to second only to Pharaoh; David, who slays Goliath; Joshua, who leads the march on Jericho; Daniel, who survives lions; Peter, the rough and blustery fisherman; and James and John, the notorious "sons of thunder." Kings, conquerors, and untamed men!

These are the kinds of muscular stories we want our sons to hear and the brand of manliness that we want them to embrace.

We shy away from men in the Bible who share the stage with strong, courageous women or who don't fit the typical hero profile that reinforces traditional patriarchal cultural values. These missing men are crucial, for they are heroically doing battle with the malestrom. Battered and bruised though they may be, they must be allowed to tell their stories. They picture for us a wiser, radically new, gospel-brand of man—incontrovertible evidence that God is at work in his world, that Jesus has come, and that his Spirit is alive and active. The *newness* of God's kingdom is breaking through, and that newness shows up in his sons, even in Old Testament times. The stories of these missing men are alive with the power and hope of the gospel, and they stand tall on the pages of Scripture, not because they satisfy the world's fallen cultural definitions of what it means to be a man, but because they reconnect with their calling as God's true sons. All of us, men and women, need these missing men if we hope to gain insight into the missing chapter.

I know this book will have its shortcomings. As a white American female who is blessed with enormous privileges, I cannot speak for men or for cultures different from my own, although I hope this book helps raise awareness of this wider world and of the crucial issues men are facing. At the same time I'm unapologetic about taking up this subject as a woman and believe a female perspective is essential. In fact, what could be more appropriate than for an *ezer*-warrior[26] to take up the cause of her brothers?

As I write, I am more convinced than ever of the urgency of expanding the discussion of God's vision for his daughters to encompass God's vision for his sons. We must dare to ask twenty-first-century questions of the Bible, no matter how taboo or unsettling they may be and with the expectation that the gospel speaks with fresh hope and purpose into men's lives today.

Walter Brueggemann's words remind us that there is always more to learn. "For the church is not permitted simply to repeat the 'old truths.' It must listen for and take a chance that from time to time the normative word is breaking through in new ways."[27] This is no mere academic debate and never has been. Current events remind us all that this is a matter of life and death.

The gospel is more than equal to these challenges—not a triumphalist American gospel that relies on prosperity—but a gospel of indestructible identity, hope, and purpose that will preach in the smoking ruins of Iraqi cities, in the slums of Nairobi, on the streets of Ferguson, Missouri, and to the utterly lost men of ISIS.

Recapturing God's global vision for men is the urgent task to which we now turn.

DISCUSSION QUESTIONS

1. What definition(s) of manhood have you heard and/or been taught and embraced?

2. What is the malestrom? What circumstances, changes, and events in today's world threaten a man or boy's sense of himself as a man according to your definition(s)?

3. How does male violence relate to this discussion?

4. Why is it important to expand our discussion of the Bible's definition of manhood into the global arena? What complexities and challenges does a global perspective create and what do we risk without it?

5. How does the malestrom challenge the church to reexamine our understanding of God's vision for his sons, and why does this include an honest discussion of patriarchy?

CHAPTER 1

THE GENESIS OF
THE MALESTROM

"This is a man's world!"
—James Brown

HISTORICALLY, MEN HAVE HAD A monopoly on positions of power and leadership in the world. They have dominated the public sphere and until recently (still in some cultures) held a virtual monopoly on education. The news is filled with their achievements, debates, and conflicts. World history and church history are largely comprised of stories of men. Even in the twenty-first century, it's still considered breaking news and something of an anomaly when a woman appears on the global stage, as happened in the 2013 election of South Korea's eighteenth president, Park Geun-hye. The big news was *not* simply that South Koreans had elected a new president and what this change means for the country's future, relations with North Korea, and international affairs. The big news was that this president is a *female*—South Korea's first—with the double distinction of being also the first *woman* to become the head of state in Northeast Asia's modern history.

Little wonder that soul singer James Brown belted out: "This is a man's world!" Evidence supports his claim. Even the Bible can give the impression that we live in "a man's world." A good 90 percent of the characters are male, and Jesus, who of course is male, used father-son terms to describe his relationship with God—which led one evangelical leader publicly to embrace James Brown theology when he confidently asserted that Christianity has "a masculine feel."[1]

Even this perception reflects the destructive presence of the malestrom, for the "man's world" mind-set is symptomatic of a world that has lost its center. The assumption that men own the stage or that the Bible gives preeminence to males over females positions men at the center. Inevitably this means men have turf to protect from each other and from women. It implies that women are to center their efforts on supporting and maintaining what God is doing through men. Women who rise to prominence today are perceived as threats; consequently, strong women in the Bible cannot be taken as exemplars for they are deemed aberrations and "exceptions to the rule."

The pervasive impact of the malestrom is as fundamental as how one sees the world. Any meaningful discussion of what it means to be male is hopelessly off track before it even starts if questions of male/female equality or who leads and who follows become the starting point. The malestrom will outwit us, and we will be thrown off in our attempts to fill in that missing chapter if we don't ground ourselves at the outset by asking the foundational question: Whose world is this?

The Bible doesn't risk the possibility of our getting off to a false start. It opens by plunging a stake in the virgin ground of Planet Earth that is the basis for understanding everything that follows, including who we are and why we are here. The Bible's story launches by proclaiming: "*In the beginning God created the heavens and the earth.*"

This statement is not mere rhetoric or tribal folklore and certainly is not meant to inspire scientific debate. In the field of higher education, scholars Jan Meyer and Ray Land have coined the phrase "*threshold knowledge*," which refers to "core concepts that once understood, transform perception of a given subject."[2] We are standing on the threshold of human history, and the Bible does not leave us guessing at whose world this is or who stands at the center.

These inaugural words anchor us "in the deepest reality about which we can speak,"[3] establishing the Creator God as the uncontested referent for all reality, including and most especially what it means to be male and female. God is at the center. Gloss over the significance of this one statement, and thereafter, everything is hurtling off course. Absolutely *nothing* is more important or definitive than words this Creator God will say about male and female. This "threshold knowledge" transforms everything else—our self-perception as well as our perception of gender. These first words are theological in the deepest sense of the term, because they center our attention first and foremost to the study of God and his ways.

The creation narrative is the first place we must go to recover the missing chapter. This is the world *before* the fall, *before* the brokenness, *before* the battle of the sexes, and *before* the malestrom began to distort, distract, diminish, and deprive men and boys from the high calling God entrusts to them.

The first two chapters of the Bible give us God's original blueprints for humanity—the purest unedited version of what God had (and still has) in mind for us and for *his* world. This text must be given primary weight in any meaningful discussion of what it means to be male or female. If we merely employ these chapters to establish basic human equality or to argue for the primacy of male over female based on whom God created first, we will miss the big vision God is casting for his image bearers. To leap forward, as many do, to construct a theology of gender based on words of a post-fall curse[4] or even on New Testament texts written thousands of years later, is to back into the subject from within the context of a fallen world. Such an approach is to attempt construction of an edifice without first laying the foundation.

The creation narrative escorts us back to the beginning—to the missing chapter and the world as God envisioned it. This is where God is defining kingdom strategies, identifying realms, and empowering all creatures great and small (and even celestial bodies) to fulfill their divine callings. This is where the Creator speaks powerful *governing statements* that define what it means to be human and that hardwire into his sons an indestructible identity, meaning, and purpose that even the malestrom is powerless to undo. Ironically, instead of diminishing Adam or any man-child born subsequently, the Bible's inaugural statement will have an extraordinary exalting effect on what it means to be a man or a woman.

CREATED IN GOD'S IMAGE

We're only one sentence into God's Story, human beings haven't even been mentioned, and already we have the first big clue in understanding what it means to "be a man." Before we even get to the creation of male and female, we have already witnessed God in creative action in ways that ultimately define and shape what it means to be human. This God is an artist. He has incomprehensible power, but he uses his power to nurture and empower others and to create a world that is conducive to their flourishing. His actions embody love, wisdom, generosity, and grace—and everything he does is utter goodness.

This staggering display of God's character and heart for the world leads up to the climactic event of God's creative genius: the creation of human beings. Human beings, we soon learn, are created *to be like this God*. We need to take a moment to try to absorb what we have just witnessed.

The pivotal importance of the creation of human beings is dramatically signaled by an abrupt halt in the action that up to this point has acquired the steady predictable rhythm of a drumbeat that shifts into drumroll. Without warning, we are drawn behind the scenes where we become privy to a divine strategic planning session and the dramatic unveiling of God's final blueprints for the human race. It is a sacred moment of unparalleled significance. No one could have seen it coming:

> Then God said, *"Let us make human beings[5] in our image, in our likeness,* so they may rule over the fish in the sea and the birds in the sky, over the livestock and all the wild animals, and over all the creatures that move along the ground. So God created human beings in his own image, in the image of God he created them; *male and female* he created them.[6]

It is unfortunate that the notion of human beings as God's image bearers has taken on the overfamiliarity of a cliché. Even in Christian circles, we toss "image bearer" language around without weighing the revolutionary visionary and missional nature of God's pronouncement. It should take our breath away to realize the enormity of the honor he bestows on us.

God's decision to create human beings in his "image and likeness" is the single most important statement about men we have. The *imago dei* is the starting point and the overarching governing presupposition for any meaningful discussion of what it means to be male. Without this radical pronouncement in the forefront of gender discussions, men are left groping in the dark for answers, taking horizontal clues from fallen cultural mores and traditions, and settling for earthbound definitions of manhood that fall appallingly short of what God envisions — definitions that render men perpetually assaulted by threats to their right to be called a man.

The *imago dei* is not a sidebar but the *centerpiece* of the discussion of who God created his sons to be. It locates male identity in an entirely different category from every other definition of manhood. Gender debates too often fail to grasp the revolutionary implications for manhood. Instead, we take sides and seize on proof texts in an attempt to defeat and diminish the arguments of opponents. The result is a stalemate and a kind of trench warfare with little hope of progress. The *imago dei* is reduced to a secondary issue instead of the essential visionary centerpiece. Editors may have had their reasons, but I find it ironic, not to mention theologically anomalous, that the classic complementarian volume whose title declares as its goal, *Recovering Biblical Manhood and Womanhood*,[7] does not get around to devoting a chapter to the *imago dei* until chapter 12.

Systematic theologians all too often turn the discussion of the *imago dei* into an abstraction. The *imago dei* is framed as a list of bullet points—of moral, spiritual, intellectual, and relational attributes that human beings have in common with God. It is the equivalent of trying to grasp a clear sense of what a man is like by studying his medical chart.

Biblical scholars point to the ancient Near Eastern practice of rulers placing statues of themselves to assert their sovereignty in regions of their realm where they were not physically present. But even while the concept may be helpful at some level, it ultimately is lacking. Statues are fixed and unchanging. Statues are to the *imago dei* what a wooden Pinocchio is to a real boy.

> What ultimately happens is that instead of being shaken by a visionary calling that will take everything we have to offer and more, we end up with a *static* list of attributes that are echoes of the divine in us. Efforts to pin down the precise meaning of image bearer (which the text does not do) ultimately box up the subject. We are sitting on the launch pad of God's vision for the world talking about nuts and bolts and heat-resistant tiles instead of buckling up for the ride of our lives. As a result, we brush right past some of the most important statements in the Bible and miss the breathtaking vista God is spreading before his daughters and his sons.[8]

God steadfastly resists this kind of thinking. The *imago dei* is not static and cannot be condensed to a list of attributes. God is not engaging in taxonomy. He isn't merely defining a new species or embedding certain qualities in men to distinguish them from other life forms. He is giving identity, meaning, and purpose to his sons and calling them to undertake a global task.

The significance of the *imago dei* is impossible to overstate, much less fully comprehend. I daresay we will spend all eternity unpacking the rich meaning involved in bearing God's image. But this much is perfectly clear already: *image bearing is not a spectator sport.* God is calling his sons to action and counting heavily on what they do. God did not create the world or his image bearers in finished form—that is to say, everything in this new world is raw, untapped, and undeveloped, and the potential for growth is immense. This grand global vision will require much of his image bearers.

Even in an unfallen world, bearing the image of the Creator was a never-ending challenge that demanded the full engagement of his sons. This calling draws their eyes God-ward to find out more about the God whose image they bear and to learn new ways of extending his reign on earth. Like the astrophysicists who probe the universe with increasingly high-powered telescopes, satellites, and interplanetary land rovers, and after thousands of years of access to information about ourselves, we are forced to admit that we are still standing on the edges of an infinite frontier—with new ground to gain and much more to learn.

MANNING UP

The Bible itself offers help on how God's sons live into their image-bearer callings. After Cain's horrible fratricide of Abel, we are told that Adam fathered a third son *"in his own likeness, in his own image; and he named him Seth."*[9] The text employs precisely the same Hebrew words that describe God's creation of human beings, only this time it describes human offspring. This provides us with a parallel that helps us flesh out the meaning of the *imago dei.*

Usually, when we speak of a son's likeness to his father, we are at the very least talking about a physical resemblance. That's what we mean when we remark, "He's the spitting image of his dad." He looks like his dad or he has a gift for music or science, just like his dad. A boy inherits these genetic likenesses to his father by birth. They're coded in his DNA.

A son inherits his father's genetic characteristics at birth. But there are characteristics a son only acquires by spending time with dad—characteristics that result from relationship, understanding, and imitation.

Nigerian attorney and American immigrant Samuel Adewusi heard his father say that "a man's true strength comes from his character." Adewusi internalized his father's words and then sought to emulate his father's example. He remarked that he often watched his father cook for his hungry family and then endure being scorned by his community for doing "women's work."[10] But Adewusi learned from his father's example that cooking for his family had nothing to do with gender roles. He was seeing his father's strong character as a man in action—an example he followed.

The *imago dei* invites this kind of familial relationship, and right from the start, God grants unparalleled access to himself by "walking in the garden"[11] where his image bearers live. Even after the fall, God's commitment to be known remains unchanged and even seems to ramp up. All creation speaks of him. He empowers prophets to speak the clear message and expose how God's *image bearers* have lost their way. Best of all, he sent Jesus—the perfect *imago dei*— "the radiance of God's glory and the *exact representation of his being*"[12]—who alone can say, "Anyone who has seen me has seen the Father."[13] What is more, we have God's Spirit as our teacher, opening our understanding and giving the courage to become part of that missing chapter and to live as citizens of a kingdom that is not of this world.

No man or boy is equal to the challenge of bearing God's

image. It will take him out of his comfort zone, raise the bar in entirely new ways, and require the power of God's Spirit as he makes God his study and resists the allure of the malestrom. Even in Eden, *before* the fall, this wasn't an easy assignment.

THE *IMAGO DEI* OVERTURNS PATRIARCHY

In contrast to patriarchy's fluctuating continuum of cultural definitions of manhood, the Bible's definition of what it means to be a man is *universal* and *unchanging*. From Adam to the present, every boy-child born into the world is the *imago dei* — already armed with his God-given identity and marching papers. He is born to know and reflect his Creator and to do God's work in the world. No man or boy is excluded. Every square inch of the earth and every season and vocation in life are encompassed in this overarching global calling.

The *imago dei* does not require rites of passage. It is a *birthright*. It *cannot* be earned. It is a gift bestowed by the Creator and hardwired into his DNA that must be lived.

> One does not have to convert to become human according to Scripture. One is born human, born with the image of God imprinted on one's soul. Every single human being on the face of the earth — from Timbuktu to Time Square, from the halls of the Church of England to the halls of Willow Creek Church, from the synagogues of Israel to the mosques of Baghdad, from the Hindu temples of India to the Buddhist temples in China — every single person on earth is made in the image of God.[14]

It is *permanent* and accompanies every male from his first breath to his last. Nothing can erase it or take it from him. He can't even shed it himself. He can ignore it, violate it, or believe he's lost it. Others may try to demean or beat it out of him, but because it is grounded in God, it is impervious to destruction. In fact, his *imago dei* identity alone means atrocities and injustices perpetuated against him take on cosmic dimensions and are an offense against the Creator himself.

The hallmarks of patriarchal masculinity—man as impregnator-protector-provider—put every man on shaky ground. These callings come with a short shelf life, even for men with a normal life expectancy and who follow that life script. They exclude young boys and won't hold up under the adversities, losses, bad choices, and contingencies of life in a fallen world. A friend of mine, firmly ensconced in patriarchy's definition—complete with a wife and five children—was tragically widowed and, like Job, bereaved of all his children. Does this mean he is less of a man now? According to patriarchy's definition, neither Jesus nor Paul ever achieved "true" manhood because they never married or produced male offspring.

Worst of all, patriarchy turns a man's focus on himself—on his abilities and authority over others. His manhood is sustained by the submission and obedience of others. Patriarchy fails to reinforce God as the center or to call a man selflessly to invest his powers and privileges to promote the flourishing and fruitful living of others. It does not beckon him to subdue the darkness and take back territory the Enemy has seized. It does not transform him into a new kind of man. Patriarchy actually prevents men from thinking in more expansive ways of what God calls them to be, the profound significance he embeds in their lives, and the impact he means for them to have on others.

In contrast to patriarchy, God's vision for his sons doesn't polarize male and female, but unites them in profound and significant ways. The Creator gives both male and female precisely the same responsibilities when he entrusts the whole earth to their rule and care. The words of Genesis 1 encompass every human being, every facet of human life, and the entire planet, and they leave every other conceivable view of men and women in the dust.

In God's scheme of things, men and women *need* each other to fulfill their purposes. The call to be fruitful and multiply involves multiplying human beings, but involves more than mere physical reproduction. These are also spiritual and theological callings. God summons his image bearers to live fruitfully as faithful stewards of the gifts, opportunities, and blessings he bestows and of the earth's vast resources. They are to live out their identity and mission as God's representatives on earth.

Genesis 2 drills down into the details as we take a closer look at the creation and the strategic kingdom relationship between male and female.

THE *EZER KENEGDO*

Adam is not singled out as an individual until Genesis 2, where the narrative zooms in to teach us more about the relationship between male and female. Again, we are witnessing sacred history—love in action—as the Creator God, the very heartbeat of the universe, bends down, scoops up a fistful of earth from which he sculpts the first man, and breathes into him "the breath of life." Humanity is not *spoken* into existence. Human beings are God's intimate, hands-on creative work of art as he literally *fleshes out* his vision for human beings to bear his image.

Although this text speaks powerfully to all of God's people, the Creator is making explicit governing statements about relations between male and female for his sons to ponder. God follows the creation of Adam with an unsettling break from his previously unanimous verdict of "It is good." This again is intended to cause readers (especially God's sons) to sit up and take notice. "It is *not good* for the man to be alone. I will make a helper [*ezer*] suitable [*kenegdo*] for him."[15]

Three important clarifications are in order: First, God creates the man at the pinnacle of his creative efforts. The man is a *masterpiece*. In creating the woman, God is not correcting a mistake or adjusting his original plans. He is implementing kingdom strategies based on the blueprints laid out in Genesis 1, which underscores the vital need for his final creative act.

Second, God doesn't explain the meaning of the man's aloneness or limit aloneness to the simple need for companionship. Nor does he identify the context in which his aloneness is a concern. This part of the narrative has relevance to but is *not* confined to marriage. The subject of marriage only is mentioned briefly as an editorial comment at the end of the chapter when the relevance to marriage is noted.[16] This editorial comment however, is remarkable for its antipatriarchal stance. Under patriarchy, a son remains under the same roof as his father, and his wife is absorbed into her husband's family. Genesis reverses this practice by instructing the man to leave his parents and unite with his wife. It goes against the patriarchal grain. But the preceding text is all-inclusive—addressing *every* human being regardless of their marital status or season of life.

Third, God is not making light of men or women by providing help for tasks men are perfectly capable of doing for themselves. Nor is God adding to a man's workload by creating a woman who needs him to protect, provide, and lead her. None of these responsibilities or roles is mentioned in the text.

If the first chapter of Genesis stresses the "good" of God's creation, this second chapter not only introduces into the narrative that which is "not good" but also the unanticipated prospect of "evil." As if the image-bearer mission God lays out in Genesis 1 and the immense spiritual challenges and global responsibilities weren't daunting enough, Genesis 2 reveals serious obstacles, and the creation mandate to "subdue" takes on a whole new meaning.

Despite the sermons we've heard, Eden was not a safe place. There are "dangerous trees"[17] and the threat of death for disobedience. The tree of the knowledge of good and evil is a harbinger that all is not well in the beautiful garden. Hidden in the shadows, like Typhon of Greek mythology, is the reptilian "father of all monsters." Other dangers seem to lurk in the shadows. God employs military language when he places Adam in the garden and instructs him "to work it and take care of [keep or guard] it."[18] The same military language is repeated later to describe the sword-wielding cherubim God stationed east of Eden to "guard" the garden after Adam and Eve are cast out.[19] The use of military language hints of possible intruders.

With these forebodings of sinister forces, it should not surprise us that God employs military language to describe the woman. The narrative uses unusually powerful words to describe her—she is *ezer kenegdo*. Robert Alter notes that *ezer kenegdo* "connotes active intervention on behalf of someone, *especially in military contexts*, as often in Psalms" (emphasis added).[20] The fact that the text describes the woman in military terms not only underscores the level of substantial help she provides, but it also alerts us that the threat level has been raised to red in the Garden of Eden.

Ezer[21] is a Hebrew noun that in the Bible always appears in a military context and is recognized as a military term. This is image-bearer language, for *ezer* is used most often in the Old Testament to refer to God as Israel's *Ezer* when his people are oppressed and suffering at the hands of their enemies.[22] So strong is the word *ezer* that Jewish parents chose it when naming their sons.[23] *Ezer* is an explicit way that God's daughters are called to image God. She is a warrior on behalf of God's kingdom and joins the man in battling the darkness, advancing God's kingdom, and watching his back.

Kenegdo is another important Hebrew descriptor that informs the reader that the woman is the man's full partner. She is neither the man's inferior nor his superior. She is his match. According to Gerhard von Rad, "The man no doubt recognized the animals which were brought to him as helps, but they were *not counterparts of equal rank.* So God moved on, in the most mysterious way, to create the woman — from the man! As distinct from the animals, she was *a complete counterpart* which the man at once recognized and greeted as such" (emphasis added).[24]

Battle lines are drawn in Eden — not between male and female or among the ranks of any of God's image bearers. The battle lines are between God's image bearers and the dark threat that the Enemy brings — between the kingdom of heaven and the kingdom of darkness. God is providing *essential* and *substantial* help without which the man cannot fulfill his God-given calling. The man *needs* the *ezer kenegdo* if he is to accomplish the purposes for which he was created.

But there is another vital reason why the man *needs* the woman, why his aloneness was so troubling to God, and why the *ezer kenegdo* provides God's perfect solution. The most glaring aspect of Adam's aloneness centered on his image-bearer calling. Adam is one. But the God he represents is plural — a Trinitarian *three in one.* A solitary image bearer cannot adequately or accurately reveal God in the world, much less fulfill his destiny as a human being. Obviously, this is a matter of grave importance to the Creator. A masculine understanding of God is woefully incomplete and actually misrepresents who God is. The consequences are disastrous. "Because we have split human qualities into polarized masculine and feminine characteristics, and projected only one sex onto God, we have a stunted sense of God's fullness."[25]

The Creator commissions the *ezer kenegdo* to reflect his image and do his work. She bears responsibility to rule and subdue creation with the man. She will share the burdens and get under the load. She enters into God's purposes for his world at the deepest level. By creating the woman, God is providing the strong ally that the man needs for the monumental challenges they face. She is uniquely called to promote his flourishing and join him in this battle. And he will do the same for her.

GOD SPLITS THE ADAM

God could easily have taken another fistful of earth to create the woman. But he does not. His method of creating the woman is profound. It avoids the possibility of any confusion and reinforces the *ezer*-warrior's rank as *kenegdo*. In an astonishing move, God creates the *ezer* from Adam's own body. The message for God's sons is utterly profound.

While the man is in a deep sleep, God removes tissue from his body and from his flesh and bones creates the woman. Many Hebrew scholars believe "a rib" is not the most accurate translation, but that God removed *"a good portion of Adam's side."*[26] This explains Adam's later pronouncement that she is "bone of my bones and flesh of my flesh; she shall be called 'woman,' for she was taken out of man."[27]

Far from polarizing male and female—as patriarchal definitions do—or highlighting gender distinctions between them (none of which are mentioned here), God's method in creating the woman unites them in a bone level solidarity. When the man sees the woman, he doesn't distinguish himself from her. He sees a reflection of himself. She is literally bone of his bones and flesh of his flesh perfectly reengineered into a woman. The oneness between God's male and female image bearers is unmistakable and utterly profound.

In Genesis 2 God is putting the finishing touches on the male/female alliance he envisioned when he drew up blueprints for the human race. He is not simply saying "both" male and female have callings, but that their calling is one. He is making a rather shocking countercultural point that his sons *need* their *ezer*-warrior sisters to become the men God created them to be and to fulfill their purpose in this world. This won't happen if they move forward without God's daughters. "It is not good for the man to be alone."

As Good As It Gets

The beautiful capstone God places on his creation is to bestow his priceless blessing on this male/female alliance[28] and to send them out to do his work together. This is accompanied by God's joyous, thunderous declaration that his creation now is "*very* good!"[29] The English rendering "very" is an understatement. The Hebrew connotation is that the creation of God's image bearers—a *blessed* male/female alliance with God at the center—is "emphatically," "exceedingly," or "forcefully" good—the grand equivalent of a divine fist bump!

One cannot escape God's delight in the creation of man and woman or the hope that exudes from his joy. The wonders of creation are breathtaking, but the clear focus of God's heart centers on his male and female image bearers. Andy Crouch wisely reminds us that the call to bear God's image "is a vocation for every human being, and whenever a human being manages to refract into the world something of the true character of the Creator God, even when they do so imperfectly and incompletely," we are witnessing "God's original grace in creation, his continuing grace in sustaining goodness in a world gone wrong, and his ultimate intentions for the cosmos."[30]

One searches in vain for patriarchy in these first two chapters. There is no hierarchy; there is no male authority over female. There is not a hint that Adam makes the final decision or that he is the spiritual leader who rules over the female or that masculinity alone adequately describes the mission God envisions. Only cultural eisegesis will lead to such conclusions.[31] The Blessed Alliance counters such misguided claims. God's image shines brightest on earth and beams back to heaven the clearest reflection of himself when his male and female image bearers join forces to align themselves with him and serve him together. This is a potent, unstoppable key kingdom strategy. Moreover, it puts his image bearers on the Enemy's radar. This strategic alliance becomes a prime Enemy target and a key to dismantling God's purposes for the world.

THE BIRTH OF THE MALESTROM

Everything collapses so fast in the biblical narrative that we hardly have time to absorb God's grand vision or the high honor he bestows on his sons and daughters before the Enemy torpedoes everything. The Enemy's first assault is beyond brilliant. With a single blow, the Enemy destroys the powerful alliance — the two foundational pillars on which God's kingdom stands: God's image bearers are cut off from their Creator and a chasm opens up between the male and the female. Instead of thriving on their life-giving relationship with God, God's image bearers go into hiding. Instead of a Blessed Alliance between male and female, the battle of the sexes commences. It is an utter disaster.

The woman is seduced by the promise of an acceleration of the *imago dei* that removes God from the center and bypasses the necessity of a relationship with him. Eat the forbidden fruit and *"you will be like God."* The woman is deceived and takes the bait. But the man is not deceived and knows exactly what he is doing when he willfully joins her in eating the fruit.[32] They stand together as they were created to do, but in this instance they stand together against God. The instant they turn away from God, the man loses his center and the malestrom is born.

Signs of the malestrom's currents are quick to surface. When God confronts Adam, he is unrepentant and instead blames the Creator and the *ezer kenegdo*. "The woman you put here with me — she gave me some fruit from the tree, and I ate it."[33] Those words of blame have managed to stick, and to this day make men distrustful of their sisters and uneasy about working together.

The gender chasm widens when God curses his errant image bearers and tells the woman that the man "will rule over" her.[34] These words become the centerpiece of patriarchal thinking and open the door, not simply for a male/female hierarchy, but also a hierarchy of men over men. Now, instead of ruling creation together, men and women turn their creation mandate against one another. The original Blessed Alliance of the man and the woman becomes tense and adversarial.

Adam downsizes the *ezer kenegdo* when he names her Eve and defines her purpose as "the mother of all the living." Lilian Barger observes that this is where "Adam begins his dysfunctional subordination of woman.... Originally created a free moral creature to rule in an expansive way with man and together fill the earth and subdue it, woman now has the boundaries of her life limited by the man."[35] Instead of jointly exercising rule over the earth, the woman's mandate is "reduced to her reproductive role." Barger, a mother herself, is quick to point out that the problem isn't Eve's calling as a mother, but rather in "having her identity reduced to it, leaving a legacy by which helping and nurturing work came to be seen as the only 'natural' place of women." [36]

The malestrom's currents swell as cultures confine women to their ability to produce sons for their husbands and patriarchy embraces a post-fall vision of male and female grounded on words of curse that men will "rule" over women. The gold standard for determining the value of a woman is no longer anchored to God and his call to bear his image and to rule and subdue alongside the man. Under patriarchy she is valued through her relationships with men — her father, husband, and especially her sons. In biblical times, a woman's value was determined by counting her sons. One of the highest accolades a woman could merit was to be "the mother of seven sons."

Pressure on men to "lead" their wives (which is how "rule" has been nuanced in western evangelical circles) means that often men aren't looking for a *kenegdo* partner who will be his strongest ally in his calling, and who will at the same time challenge him when he veers from God's purposes. After the fall, masculinity is defined in terms of male leadership over others. Men are now looking to control women.

The cost to God's kingdom is incalculable. The alliance has lost its divine center. Women become dependent and shrink back even in the face of kingdom battles. The rich reflection of God's character becomes distorted. Trinitarian oneness they were created to reflect fractures, and the body of Christ is limping. The Enemy gets a reprieve from the creation mandate.

"Patriarchy was never God's intention, but a manifestation, or consequence, of human sin. The rule of men and the disastrous effects it has on women *and men* are a result of rebellion against God and God's intended order" (emphasis added).[37] Cultures, religions, and churches usurp God's prerogative as Creator and exceed their proper bounds when they devise, impose, and enforce inferior definitions of masculinity on men and boys. God has never given up on his original vision and will not abandon his sons to the dangerous swirling malestrom. The God who "in the beginning ... created the heavens and the earth" will not be denied and in the end will have his way.

James Brown theology definitely misses the mark. But we are mistaken if we dismiss patriarchy altogether, for it serves a crucial purpose. *Patriarchy matters* because it is the best cultural backdrop to teach us the Bible's message. Again, it is *not* the Bible's message, but a teaching tool God has chosen to open our eyes to the "not of this world" nature of the kingdom of heaven of which we are citizens. This cultural backdrop is no more powerfully effective than in the story of the ultimate patriarch, Father Abraham. Abraham's story enters the battle by taking us into the malestrom's vortex where the gospel confronts patriarchy head-on.

DISCUSSION QUESTIONS

1. Why is it important to begin the discussion of manhood with the creation narrative (Genesis 1–2) and especially with the "threshold knowledge" of Genesis 1:1?

2. How does the overarching vision of human beings—male and female—as God's image bearers trump all other views of masculinity? How does the *imago dei* vision surpass patriarchy?

3. How does the *imago dei* calling redefine a man or boy's mission in life? What are his priorities?

4. Who is the *ezer kenegdo* and why is she needed? How is God's creation of her instructive, and how does it transform all relationships between males and females and point toward a Blessed Alliance?

5. How did the fall birth the malestrom, and what are the effects on men?

CHAPTER 2

PATRIARCHY MATTERS

*"Things are not always what they seem;
the first appearance deceives many."*
— Phaedrus

THERE IS A PLACE IN modern-day Albania where women live as men. They are the *burrneshas* (translated "he-she"), a small and declining segment of the female population in the Alps of Northern Albania. One frustrated journalist investigating *burrneshas* remarked that finding them is "like searching for unicorns."[1]

Until recently, these sworn virgins were a secret unknown even to other Albanians who live in that region. Like the daughters of Zelophehad who sought a legal loophole in Mosaic inheritance laws when their father died without a son,[2] *burrneshas* offered families a way around patrilineal ("father-line")[3] inheritance practices when the family patriarch died without a male heir by providing a stand-in for the missing male heir.

> If a virgin daughter remained, she could assume the role of patriarch by swearing in front of a dozen village elders that she would remain celibate for the rest of her life. By this declaration, the *burrnesha* secured the family estate — and honor. It was ... "a choice of force, not happiness," a social construct and selfless act to protect the family.[4]

From that day on she would live, dress, and work as a man and would "assume the burdens and" (not to be minimized) also "the liberties of a man."[5]

According to estimates only around a hundred *burrneshas* are still living. But today, *burrneshas* take vows of celibacy and embrace the lifestyle of a male for different reasons than in the past. One modern *burrnesha* explained why she continued to live as a "he."

> Imagine ... marrying at the age of 15, 16, 17 years old, conceivably to a husband who might be 40, 50, 60. On your wedding night, your father might slip a bullet into your suitcase, for your husband's use in case you're not a virgin. You will stand throughout your wedding, eyes downcast as the humble, heeled animal you've just become, and soon you will live with your husband's family, wherever they may live, in virtual enslavement, taking all of your orders from them. You will never talk back. You will make no decision, even when it comes to the children to whom you give birth. You will not smoke or drink or shoot a gun. From sunup to sundown, your life will be full of hard labor. According to the Kanun:[6] "A woman is known as a sack made to endure as long as she lives in her husband's house."[7]

The *burrnesha's* vow offers an escape hatch from the destiny that patriarchal society assigns to women and an entrée into the status, freedoms, and agency of men. The choice is not prompted by gender identity confusion, but is a deliberate decision to avoid the fate of life as female. Of course there is a price to pay for this decision, but costly as the choice might be (for *burrneshas* can be lonely), the benefits outweigh the sacrifice.

Women aren't the only ones who need an escape hatch from patriarchy. Although patriarchy tends to favor men and confer by default privileges and authority over women, it by no means benefits all men. There is only limited space at the top of the human power pyramid. Many men spend their entire lives hopelessly trapped at the bottom—trampled and exploited by other men or by disadvantaging circumstances of birth. Ironically, patriarchy even poses serious hazards to men who seem at first glance to benefit most from this social arrangement. They may live their entire lives ensconced in the status, power, and privilege patriarchy bestows on men, but that may be exactly what leaves them vulnerable to the more subtle dangers of the malestrom.

Millennial males in the West are increasingly resisting patriarchal confines or simply finding unworkable the roles and rules imposed on them by traditional patriarchal views and suspicious of the motives involved. As Christian Piatt observes,

> The notion of a set of norms, rules, or values that apply to many of us seem arbitrary and desperate at best. At worst, it smacks of the kind of colonialist oppression from which many of us have endeavored to emerge.... And really, when we talk nostalgically about the loss of traditional cultural roles, the only ones usually mourning such changes are those who directly benefited from things as they were.[8]

At a time when patriarchy is in decline and increasingly deemed passé in progressive western cultures like our own, when global opposition to patriarchal tenets is mounting as gains in education and human rights empower women and girls and male/female relationships become more egalitarian, the subject of patriarchy remains a powerful global issue. Despite these cultural changes, it persists as a divisive topic in evangelical circles in large part because patriarchy is on virtually every page of the Bible. The question is not whether the Bible contains patriarchy, but does the Bible affirm and require patriarchy for the followers of Jesus?

For insight, we turn to the patriarch of the patriarchs— Abraham.

THE CALL OF THE PATRIARCH

In 1939, at the beginning of World War II, England's King George VI borrowed the words of poet Minnie Louise Haskins to reassure a worried nation as they faced a frightening uncertain future. "Go into the darkness and put your hand into the hand of God. That shall be to you better than light and safer than a known way!"

Those words are an apt description of the journey that commenced when God called Abraham to follow him into the great unknown. "Go from your country, your people and your father's household to the land I will show you."[9] When Abraham received the call from God, the world was recklessly out of step with the Creator. The catastrophic flood demonstrated the terrible peril humanity was ignoring. Pressed against the history of a fallen humanity, hope breaks through when God issues this call to Abraham. This is the glorious moment when winter's ice and snow begin melting and rumors spread that "Aslan is on the move!" God has not turned his back on his people. He is bending down and reengaging his image bearers, starting over — this time with the seventy-five-year-old patriarch. And in an act of uncommon trust (the moment readers should exhale with relief), Abraham put his hand into the hand of God and began his walk of faith into the dark unknown.

Readers miss the full significance of this call of the patriarch if we do not recognize that Abraham is not following the patriarchal script. For a son to step away from the world that promised him so much as his father's firstborn, his obedience to God marks an overt disavowal of patriarchal norms. By calling Abraham to leave his father and his father's legacy behind, God is calling Abraham to abandon patriarchy. The call of the Creator has priority over the cultural standards of the day. Starting with Abraham, God is creating a new people whose parameters exceed bloodlines and cultural privileging and whose impact on the world will be blessings to others—goodness, fruitfulness, and flourishing.

The call of the patriarch to leave his father is not the last time God will command him to be countercultural. This call will require trusting God in circumstances far more challenging than leaving Haran. It will mean going to the brink of his faith to violate his deepest patriarchal instincts when God asks him to do the inconceivable and offer up Isaac, his long-awaited treasured and only son of promise. God will go against the grain of everything that makes sense in the patriarchal world Abraham must leave behind to follow God into this unknown future. Walter Brueggemann captures the newness represented by Abraham's call: "The faith of Abraham is not in anything he sees in the world, but in a word which will overcome the barrenness of the world.... The ones who are barren and hopeless become the practitioners of faith. They are the ones who do not doubt the promise and so allow the new age to surge upon them."[10]

God's call to Abraham is one of those moments in the Bible when we, as readers, set foot on holy ground.

God's covenant with Abraham mushrooms beyond all expectations—"extending far beyond Abraham and his biological descendants, moving through time into eternity, and breaking through all sorts of barriers to achieve the impossible."[11] Abraham becomes the father of both his physical descendants and the faithful from other races who inherit his faith in God. This comes with a name change for the old patriarch that is more fitting with his new calling. "No longer will you be called Abram ['exalted father']; your name will be Abraham ['father of many'], for I have made you a father of *many nations*. I will make you *very fruitful*; I will make *nations* of you, and kings will come from you."[12]

God calls Abraham and his descendants to go against culture, tribal, family, and peer pressure, and even the urges of their own hearts. Abraham is called to defy the downward currents of the malestrom and follow the Creator.

THE POWER OF PATRIARCHY

Because of the cultural distance, it is difficult for moderns to understand the full significance of Abraham leaving his father and his family. I gained some unexpected insight into the power of patriarchy one Sunday afternoon at lunch with a Tanzanian seminary student. During our conversation, I casually asked what it was like to be the firstborn son in his family. Nothing prepared me for the sudden physical transformation that came over him. His shoulders straightened, and he held his head a little higher, becoming almost regal in his demeanor.

"I am my father's confidant," he replied, his eyes aglow with evident pride. "My father makes no decision without first consulting me." He went on to describe how his siblings esteem him and defer to his leadership. At his birth, his father gave his own name to him—twice. "Kitula Kitula" bore the double honor due the eldest son. He is the pride of his family and the promise of their future. As a son, he will carry on his father's name, build his father's house, and inherit his father's wealth. Kitula's story gives insight into the patriarchal world and a sense of what Abraham left behind when he departed from Haran.

Listening to Kitula that day left an indelible impression on me and transformed how I read the word "son" in the Bible, especially of Jesus as the Father's one and only beloved Son. Kitula shed new light on the desperate quest for sons that reduces a woman's mission in life to birthing sons for her husband and where her value as a woman is measured by how many she produces. Still today in Kitula's Tanzania, a woman who doesn't bear sons for her husband will be "in trouble." Her husband will divorce her or add another wife, although Kitula hastened to add these practices are declining among Christians. He illumined new dimensions of agony and danger to women in the Bible (like Sarah, Rebekah, Rachel, and Hannah), who endured shameful years of barrenness. If we do not understand the patriarchal context, we will miss, distort, or trivialize the Bible's message. Although it was not his intention, Kitula reminded me that the Bible is not an American book.

Patriarchy is one of the many keys that unlock the deeper riches of the Bible, but there is a dark side to patriarchy too that we dare not ignore. Romanticizing aspects of patriarchy means glossing over the horrific dangers this cultural system poses to women and girls, as recorded in the Bible and reported by today's media. But patriarchy is not merely proving unworkable in the lives of many women today; it is just as harmful and destructive to men—both in ancient times and now.

THE DARK SIDE OF PATRIARCHY

Abraham was a man of extraordinary faith who deserves to be admired and emulated for many reasons. But Abraham himself was also a man of his time. His entanglements in patriarchal customs put him on a trajectory that was at cross-purposes with God's call on his life. God's dealings with Abraham will compel him to rethink what kind of man he is and how, as a man privileged with power, he regards others.

God's covenant with Abraham will ultimately summon the old patriarch back to the *imago dei* vision God was casting for men in the beginning. His story—the good, bad, and ugly of it—is a gift to those who follow Abraham as the father of the faith. He was a learner all his life, and none of the lessons he absorbed came easily.

At the ripe old age of ninety-nine, Abraham will hear words from God's mouth that require him to rethink his entire life as well as his views of God—barriers that often stand in the way of progress for those of us who can't face the possibility that we've gotten a lot of things wrong. Abraham's thoroughly patriarchal story will deliver a lethal blow against the roots of patriarchy and set in sharp relief a radical new kingdom definition of manhood that foreshadows the gospel of Jesus. But the road to that life-changing U-turn is riddled with blind spots that Abraham will spend the rest of his days sorting through. A glance through his resume reveals the soul-destroying malestrom of patriarchy in Abraham's life and how far Abraham's journey must take him.

By the time we get to Abraham's story, patriarchy is entrenched in the biblical narrative. Instead of sharing responsibility with men according to Genesis 1–2, women have become incidental to male stories, designated to produce sons to perpetuate their husband's name. Male authority over women becomes a hallmark of patriarchy. Indeed, that is precisely the meaning of patriarchy.

If patriarchy drives a wedge between men and women, primogeniture drives a wedge between brothers, often sparking deep jealousy, fierce sibling rivalry, and sometimes bloody violence. It is the story of Cain and Abel playing out again and again. Primogeniture confers birthrights and near royalty on the firstborn son. A man's first son held primacy over his younger brothers that entitled him to his father's double blessing and inheritance (meaning he inherited twice as much as his brothers). If the firstborn son was deceased, the dead man's sons took precedence over his surviving brothers.

Primogeniture is "the linchpin of an entire social and legal system" that necessarily results in "disadvantage" for most males.[13] It produces hostilities among Abraham's sons, grandsons, and great-grandsons and shapes the narratives of subsequent generations. Powerful tensions erupt between Ishmael and Isaac. Esau and Jacob become embroiled in a rivalry that threatens to become deadly and forces Jacob to run for his life. Primogeniture produces multigenerational dysfunction among Jacob's twelve sons.

The dark side of patriarchy is painfully evident in Abraham

himself. If we are honest, we must admit that Abraham was a human trafficker. He *owned* human beings—slaves he "bought," slaves given to him as "gifts,"[14] and slaves "born in his household" (which means he took ownership of children born to his slaves).[15] Slavery was an accepted practice within patriarchy and is a common but hideous thread that winds through stories of leading figures in the Bible. That fact alone is enough to give us pause about patriarchy.

But there are other reasons too. *Twice* Abraham used his wife Sarah as a human shield. He jeopardized her morally to save his own skin. Driven by the fear that other more powerful men—Egypt's Pharaoh and King Abimelech—might kill him to possess his beautiful wife, he instructed Sarah to say she was his sister and conceal the fact that she was his wife. It was a half-truth (she was his half-sister, the daughter of his father but of a different mother), but a lie nonetheless. The deception worked, at least for Abraham. But things backfired horribly for Sarah, who was abducted by both men. "Leading Old Testament experts believe that while Abimelech never touched her, a straightforward reading of the text seems to confirm that Pharaoh's conduct toward her was anything but innocent. Pharaoh reproached Abraham for deceiving him. "Why did you say, 'She is my sister,' so that *I took her to be my wife?*"[16] Sarah was sacrificed to male power and rape to protect her cowardly brother-husband.

There is more. After years of barrenness, Sarah and Abraham commandeered her slave girl Hagar as a surrogate to produce a son by Abraham for Sarah. Hagar—most likely a young teenage girl—is forced to marry a man in his eighties. This polygamous arrangement (another acceptable practice within the patriarchy of their time, but profoundly abusive of Hagar) produced the desired son, but brought endless grief down on the house of Abraham and inflicted abuse and suffering on his second wife and her son, Ishmael. Patriarchy has a dark side indeed.

PATRIARCHY UNDONE

The years my family lived in Oxford, England, were life-changing for all three of us, and I wouldn't trade them for anything. But to be honest, the whole time we were there I longed for the day when we would pack up and move back home to the States. Most of my friends shared that sentiment. We were all eager to return to our country of origin and threw parties for each other when the dissertation was successfully defended and one of us was moving home. We looked forward to the day when friends would celebrate us.

But two of my friends didn't share our enthusiasm for leaving. Both came from worlds very different from mine and from the life we all enjoyed in England. One was a Muslim from Pakistan; the other a Hindu from India. Both were intelligent, educated, and articulate. One had earned a PhD. Both came from patriarchal cultures. Both were successful mothers of sons. Yet both expressed serious dread as their time in Oxford neared a close and they contemplated returning home. Why? Because "home" meant living with their husband's family where they would come under the thumb of their mother-in-law and be treated as a child. Patriarchy was no picnic for these educated and talented women.

My two friends would have been dumbfounded to read the words in Genesis that follow God's creation of the *ezer kenegdo* and ushers her into marriage. "For this reason a man will *leave his father and mother and be united to his wife*, and they will become one flesh."[17] This is not just a romantic statement about marriage that gets repeated in wedding ceremonies in our western culture. Within the patriarchal world where a man's wife becomes family property, this one sentence in the Bible violates patriarchal tradition and dismantles it.

The Bible is replete with examples where patriarchy is rejected. Regarding the rights of the firstborn, God repeatedly transforms power relations to invalidate patriarchal priorities. It happens in stories when God bypasses the firstborn and chooses a younger brother to inherit his covenant promises. God chooses Abel and then Seth, not Cain; Isaac, not Ishmael; Jacob, not Esau. Jacob favors Rachel's sons, Joseph and Benjamin (sons eleven and twelve), over their older brothers, but the kingly line goes to Judah, Leah's fourth son. And when Jacob blesses Joseph's sons, he gives the greater blessing to Ephraim, not his older brother Manasseh despite Joseph's protests.

Patriarchy is the cultural background against which God reveals the newness of his kingdom breaking through as he overturns cultural norms that issued from the fall of Adam and Eve. In the final analysis, the gospel and the kingdom of God are not endorsements for any world system that is familiar to us in this world. Jesus is making something new — recovering that missing chapter and the kingdom we lost sight of in the fall.

We are mistaken to try to salvage pieces of a fallen human system like patriarchy. And while some readers may think this means egalitarianism wins out, even that system doesn't go far enough. David Fitch captures the problems with how we talk about these issues and the challenge for the gospel when he writes:

> The New Testament church is not about whether women should be "over" men or men "over" women. It is about eliminating the "over" entirely. It is about abolishing the politics of anybody being over anybody.... Too often however the complementarian/egalitarian logic thwarts this dynamic. "Complementarian" approaches to leadership keep hierarchy (and thereby patriarchy) in place. "Egalitarian" approaches to leadership often (unintentionally) become the means to ensconce "male dominant" ways/structures of leadership and then invite women into them.[18]

So if we are settling for systems that fall short of the mark, what does the Bible put in its place?

FROM PATRIARCH TO NEW MAN

In a move that is emphatically male and seems to exclude women and that New Testament apostles later declared non-essential, God institutes male circumcision as the sign of his covenant with Abraham.[19] God commanded Abraham and all his male descendants eight days old and older to be circumcised. This not only applied to every one of Abraham's biological descendants, but also to Abraham's servants and slaves—both those born in his household and those he purchased from foreigners. Surely Abraham was shocked to learn that the new identity was beyond ethnicity or tribe. It was a sign that pointed to a new plane of existence.

Circumcision was not new. Other tribes circumcised their males, but nowhere else did circumcision carry the weighty significance God gave it for Abraham and others he circumcised. Other cultures used male circumcision as a painful rite of passage that transitioned boys into men. Not so in Israel. Eight-day-old baby boys were circumcised and they weren't transitioning to manhood. Circumcision was "legally incumbent upon all generations. God is speaking to those who are not yet born."[20] In Israel, young boys would never recall a time when they were *un*circumcised.

Why would God choose this explicitly male rite to remind his sons of his covenant with them?

By itself, circumcision could easily (and eventually did) become an end in itself. Like the team logo that fans wear proudly on caps and T-shirts but can't explain where the symbol originated or what it meant originally, over time Jewish circumcision lost its distinctive meaning. It morphed into a national trademark adrift from its roots—a way of distinguishing Jews from Gentiles, an identifying "us versus them" marker. This is at least part of the reason New Testament apostles shifted from circumcision to embrace baptism as the new sign of God's covenant.

Circumcision of Abraham and the males in his household was a painful and permanent reminder that they were in covenant with God who called them to "Walk before me faithfully and be blameless."[21] This was God's radical restatement of what it means to be a new kind of man in a patriarchal culture—or any culture for that matter. God was reasserting what he said in the beginning, when he declared his sons to be his image bearers—a calling lost when men derive their identities and purpose from cultural systems.

God insists on a permanent physical sign to remind Abraham and his male descendants that they live under the gaze of God. Circumcision strips the malestrom and human culture of its power to define a man's identity and purpose. God created the man, and God alone defines him. The definition he bestows is indestructible because it is rooted in God himself.

Let there be no mistake here. God isn't affirming patriarchy. He is defining a whole new counter-patriarchal strategy for men who live within the patriarchal system. Yahweh is implementing kingdom changes by beginning with his sons, who have the power to open doors for others.

Circumcision, in the first place, is *not* an affirmation of male power and priority, but a transformation of both. The act of circumcision doesn't glorify male power; it awakens a man to his vulnerability. The rite of circumcision disables a man as he heals. In one of the darkest chapters of the Bible, Abraham's great grandsons Simeon and Levi abused the rite to give themselves a military advantage over the men of Shechem, who became defenseless when they agreed to circumcise themselves.[22]

By addressing men explicitly within patriarchy, God is addressing male power. Power in any form is a dangerous responsibility. It can be used for good or evil. Coupled with arrogance, anger, blind ambition, or selfishness, power in the hands of a man who has lost sight of his Creator is lethal. It may even deceive a man into thinking he's in the right when he is lording over others. Tragically in the church among the people who claim to follow Jesus, men wield power "in the name of God" while abusing others or by protecting those who abuse. God's covenant breaks up cronyism and power mongering by reminding men of their weaknesses and vulnerability.

Second, although circumcision is private and concealed beneath a man's clothing, he will encounter this covenant reminder every day. "Every time he looks at his body he is reminded that he is part of Yahweh's covenant ... a mnemonic sign, reminding God's people of who they are."[23] Every time he dresses, bathes, relieves himself, or approaches a woman, he is confronted with the reminder that he is *not* to be like other men.

He may have power, but that power is not an entitlement. It is a gift God entrusts for good and to bless. God's first words to Abraham included the promise that he and his descendants were to be a blessing to the world. That promise takes on a whole new meaning when circumcision informs how a man lives before the face of God in his private conduct, his character, and his interactions with others. He knows he's being watched. God's hand is on his sons, and Yahweh's very reputation is on the line in how his sons live.

Around men like that, *burrneshas* could embrace their God-given femaleness and would be able to thrive as women. Albanian he-she unicorns would become extinct. Slaves would breathe the free air of dignity, wholeness, empowerment, and opportunity. And men with power would flourish as God's image bearers in ways that would shock the world and give signals that there truly is a God in heaven who loves his sons and whose kingdom is not of this world. The Creator summons them to defy the downward spiral of the malestrom and rise to new heights as God's image bearers.

Circumcision also speaks of a man's wife—the *ezer*-warriors he needs to become the man God created him to be—and of their union in reproducing physically and spiritually. It speaks of his children. Not just progeny who up to now have been the focus, but the call to raise up an entirely new race of people who *"walk before God faithfully and are blameless."* It is the call for men to engage in God's creation call to be fruitful by multiplying image bearers of the living God—an impossible but vital task, for no human being can change a person's heart. Abraham is called both to model for his children a brand of manhood that isn't like what they'll see in other men and to devote himself to the nurture of their souls toward God. He will need plenty of *ezer kenegdo* help in this impossible but hopeful task.

Circumcision also flattens the human social pyramid and calls for a new kind of inclusive and richly diverse community that encompasses male and female, but expands in all directions. I can only imagine Abraham's double take when God included his slaves in the covenant—spreading the same covenant dignity, honor, and responsibilities laterally to them. How would that change how Abraham viewed the people he had purchased along with cattle and sheep? God is turning Abraham's patriarchal paradigm on its head. Illusions of superiority and inferiority have no place in the kingdom of God. Already God's covenant is defying gender, cultural, ethnic, national, and economic distinctions and boundaries. This is a foreign language to patriarchy. It is the long-forgotten ethos of God's kingdom lost in Eden, but this is God's call to the new man.

Abraham has not simply reached a pivotal moment in his own journey. This is a key event in God's purposes for the world. I fear we keep walking past it as though it was a message for another time. Circumcision is a message for today. Just to make sure Abraham doesn't forget, God etches in his body—cuts in the flesh of a man's reproductive organ—a permanent reminder of his covenant and a definition of a new kind of man.

THE CITY OF GOD

Abraham was a work in progress. His story doesn't come with a happy ending where he sees the fulfillment of all God's covenant promises. And Abraham himself would always be flawed and would still make massive blunders. His story ends with a comma, not a period.

The old patriarch reached an all-or-nothing point with Yahweh when Yahweh asked Abraham to sacrifice his son Isaac. The pride and joy of patriarchy is a man's firstborn son. But this son is Abraham's only son now—the long-awaited crowning blessing of Abraham's old age and the hope of all God's promises.

I cannot explain God's demand of Abraham or Abraham's determined obedience. But at least part of the probing of the mysteries here needs to include the fact that Abraham as never before is walking away from the malestrom's claims by his willingness—not to protect the son he waited for all his life—but to give him up if God requires. The deep, unexplained bewildering mysteries of this desperate scene notwithstanding, this is *the ultimate anti-patriarchal statement*. At the same time this is where patriarchy proves its powers to help us grasp more of the truth of the gospel and glimpse God's heart for us. At the very least, in this chapter of Abraham's story patriarchy sheds an entirely new light on the terrible heart-searing cost to God in giving up his one and only beloved Son for the world he loves and is determined to save. Any parent will find it difficult to read this part of Abraham's story. But within the patriarchal world—where a man's firstborn is his pride and joy and where an only son is a man's lifeline to the future—the pain of loss reaches unimaginable depths.

The malestrom doesn't hold Abraham's heart anymore. Yahweh does. Somewhere along the way Abraham's longings changed. He acquired a holy discontent with things as they are. The writer to the Hebrews tells us later that this great man of faith set his sights on that new world that God is restoring.

Abraham *longed* for that missing chapter. Instead of counting stars and grains of sand, he died "looking forward to the city with foundations, whose architect and builder is God." Abraham and his descendants "did not receive the things promised; they only saw them and welcomed them from a distance, admitting that they were foreigners and strangers on earth ... longing for a better country—a heavenly one. Therefore God is not ashamed to be called their God, for he has prepared a city for them."[24]

What is easy to miss in reading the Old Testament is that beginning in Genesis—in the early moments of a fallen world—the stronger currents of the kingdom of God are already overpowering the patriarchal currents of the malestrom and making way for the new things God is doing in the world he loves. In the meantime, God is still leaving clues that point his sons back to creation—back to that original vision, back to himself. This isn't a call to the past, but into the future. The journey this entails is not for the faint of heart. God's dealings with Abraham equip men to battle the malestrom and to stand against its forceful currents, even when that means standing alone.

The downward drag of human culture, of flattered egos, and self-serving power plays to the malestrom's strengths. God calls his sons to battle those forces. He doesn't offer simple answers to the challenges facing men then or now. He calls his sons to think, to question, to struggle, and to work out the details in their own stories. There is no formula. Men's lives are not all the same. But God is in the business of raising up more new men for the city of God.

The next three chapters tell the stories of malestrom combatants, sons of Abraham who join with *ezer*-warriors to defeat the malestrom's powers and who display the gospel in a brand of manhood that God uses to bless the world. The first man is Abraham's great-grandson Judah, who gets swept into a malestrom current that brings a lot of men down. Judah is pulled under by the Father Wound.

DISCUSSION QUESTIONS

1. What is patriarchy? Why is patriarchy problematic to men as well as to *burrneshas*?

2. In Abraham's story, how does God's call challenge the old patriarch's life script and how does Abraham begin to change?

3. How does circumcision as the sign of God's covenant speak of the new kind of man God is calling Abraham to be and to reproduce?

4. God's call required seventy-five-year-old Abraham to rethink his entire life, his culture, and his ultimate longings. How important is it to follow Abraham's lead in this respect?

5. How did Abraham battle the malestrom, and what does his story teach us about God's calling on his sons?

CHAPTER 3

THE FATHER WOUND

*"He never had the chance to hear his father say,
'I love you' and to say those words back."*

WHEN GRIEF WAS AT ITS rawest following the shooting death of former Beatle John Lennon, his close friend photographer Bob Gruen reflected on the difficult and at times nonexistent relationship Lennon had with his son Julian. A single bullet slammed the door shut on opportunities to close the distance between Lennon and his firstborn son. Julian Lennon was born in 1963 on the eve of Beatlemania—which put the Liverpool Lads in the spotlight and on the road and Julian and his mother Cynthia under wraps. Beatles handlers worried that screaming fans wouldn't scream as wildly for a married man with a child.

When Julian was five, his father divorced his mother to marry Yoko Ono. John and Yoko moved to New York City in 1971, putting an ocean between John and the eight-year-old son he hardly knew. Looking back, Julian lamented, "I knew life without him more than with him."

At forty, John Lennon (who had his own deep father wound) had an epiphany: a passion to be the dad he never knew—the dad he never was to Julian. So when Yoko gave birth to son number two (Sean Lennon), John threw himself into parenting. "I looked after the baby and I made the bread and I was a house husband and I'm proud of it. And it was an enlightening experience for me, because it was a complete reversal of my whole upbringing."

Watching his father's newfound devotion to his younger brother Sean, Julian mused wistfully, "Why couldn't that have happened for me?"

OUT OF A WHISKEY BOTTLE ON A SATURDAY NIGHT

The father wound is a recurrent theme in many books about men. Contemporary observers of our postmodern culture lament the lack of a "life script" to map out the route to "real" manhood, the absence of rites of passage to notify a boy (and signal to everyone else) that he's earned the right to be called a man. But the lion's share of blame for struggles adult men experience seems to center on fathers who've gone missing in action or have been a destructive presence in their son's lives. Old Testament patriarchs had father wounds too, as the dysfunctional life of Judah sadly portrays.

Wounds caused by a distant, emotionally unavailable, physically absent, or abusive father run deep and leave a gaping hole behind that can, like an unseen congenital defect, diminish the quality of a man's life or escalate over time into something worse. The father wound can be the driving force in a man's life—for good or ill. It can be the making of the man who resolves to do things differently from his dad or morph into a seething rage that transfers the pain to others and repeats the cycle.

The father wound forms a powerful malestrom undertow with such a devastating global reach it warrants the label "epidemic." Based on years of ministry to men Richard Rohr describes this wound as "so deep and so all-pervasive in so many parts of the world that its healing could well be the most radical social reform conceivable," to which he adds this frightening conclusion, "I am convinced that the father wound lies at the bottom of much crime, militarism, competitive greed, pathological need for leaders and family instability."[1] Who knows how many father wounds are underneath today's violent headlines?

The father wound has touched down in the lives of men I know. My husband, Frank, tells the story of traveling together with his seminary colleagues in a van when the conversation and the tone shifted. They began talking about their dads. Frank will never forget the wounded comment from one colleague: "When my father died, I felt nothing." His father never beat or abused him. But there was simply no emotional connection between father and son. Even seminary professors have father wounds.

Most agree that a father's voice speaks into his son's life with an unequaled significance. A father's affirmation can outweigh anyone else's criticism. One piercing jab can last a lifetime. To this day, Julian Lennon still winces when he recalls his father telling him he had "come out of a whiskey bottle on a Saturday night."

Such words can leave a lasting wound, but even a father's silence cuts deep. Wes Yoder writes, "I know many men who have never heard their fathers say, 'I love you. I'm proud of you. You're the best son a dad could ever want,' but the longing to hear those words never dies."[2]

PATRIARCHY AND PRIMOGENITURE

If you look carefully at the family stories in Genesis, you will find that the father wound is a major theme. Patriarchy has an uncanny knack for inflicting father wounds, which are exacerbated by the expectations and coveted privileges that primogeniture bestows on sons. In this male-dominated social system, daughters rarely ranked high on a father's radar, for daughters didn't have the same value as sons. With few exceptions, they don't show up in the story either—at least not often as agents of action. That doesn't mean they didn't suffer deep father wounds too. The Genesis narrator informs us that Jacob had "daughters."[3] Leah's daughter Dinah is the only daughter named when she disappoints her mother's quest for the coveted honor of bearing seven sons[4] and later when Shechem the Hivite rapes her.[5] Modern scholars have noted that after the rape Jacob "shows no moral indignation and wants only to settle the matter prudently."[6] Surely Dinah felt the pangs of his indifference.

But patriarchy turns the spotlight on sons. A man's stature in the community increased with the head-count of his sons. Primogeniture meant (as Kitula explained earlier) that the first-born son was something of a crown prince in the family. But God refuses to be held captive to the way human life is arranged and constantly overthrows it, for his kingdom doesn't embrace this kind of pecking order. Primogeniture is a prime example. Jesus stated in no uncertain terms "the first will be last."[7] The countercultural significance of such a statement would not go unnoticed by patriarchal listeners. But long before Jesus, God was already inverting the human order of things.

The "iron law of primogeniture"[8] is one of the first and central pillars of the patriarchal system that the biblical narrative demolishes. Even today primogeniture is a major argument used to bolster patriarchal thinking in the church concerning male leadership and male/female relationships. The fact that "God created Adam first" is seen as a biblical warrant for male priority over female. But as we mentioned earlier, God is no respecter of primogeniture, and with astonishing regularity inverts it to carry his purposes forward with a second or third or eleventh son. Somehow, the message goes unheeded among the patriarchs who, instead of defying culture and becoming a new brand of men, cling to patriarchal power and prerogatives. Consequently, and without skipping a beat, the claims of primogeniture and the favoritism of fathers march forward to create destructive tensions between brothers that can turn deadly.

Patriarchy begets patriarchy and father wounds beget father wounds. Isaac's partiality ignites a fierce rivalry between his twin sons, Esau and Jacob. Their rivalry is fueled by the culturally subversive prophetic oracle God revealed to their mother,

Rebekah, when the boys were still in utero that "the older will serve the younger."[9]

Primogeniture, the "linchpin" of patriarchy, cements the rights and privileges of one son over and above his brothers—in this case the rights of Esau over Jacob. But the prophecy revealed to Rebekah disrupts the culture's way of bestowing privilege and power. God chooses to carry the Abrahamic promises forward through Jacob. "This narrative, then, is a radically revolutionary announcement. It dares to call into question a conventional settlement of power."[10]

The twins' rivalry becomes life threatening when Jacob deceptively absconds with his older brother's firstborn rights to their father's blessing—a blessing Isaac was determined to bestow on his beloved Esau. When Jacob's deception is discovered, Esau threatens to kill him, forcing Jacob to run for his life, taking his brother's stolen blessing with him.

One would think the exiled Jacob would have an epiphany like John Lennon's and become the father he never had. But Jacob recycles the sins of his father to his sons by playing favorites too. Frightening, deadly consequences follow that echo the Cain and Abel struggle and where male competition and the quest for primacy make the conflict between Esau and Jacob look like child's play.

DESCENT INTO MALESTROM

Although all of Jacob's sons become embroiled in the conflict that ultimately tears the family apart, the story centers mainly on two sons. Joseph, son number eleven, commands the spotlight and is Jacob's (and most readers') favorite of the twelve. Judah is Jacob's fourth born, a dark, even sinister figure who is caught up in outrage and jealousy of Joseph and whose festering father wound drives him into the mouth of the malestrom.

Primogeniture becomes a leading cast member in this tragic

saga, like Tolkien's "Wormtongue"[11] whispering from the sidelines the patriarchal cultural rules of the game that play havoc with Jacob's wives (he ends up with four and has a favorite) and his twelve sons. Favoritism and neglect leave a trail of dysfunction, wounded souls, and criminal activity.

Before Judah was even born, he was doomed for a father-love-deprived future when his father, Jacob, was duped into marrying his mother, Leah, instead of her beautiful younger sister, Rachel. The first time Jacob laid eyes on Rachel, it was love at first sight. It's hard to fathom his terrible "morning after" regret on discovering the woman he worked seven years to marry and made passionate love to the night before wasn't Rachel, but her older, less attractive sister, Leah.

Outraged, Jacob confronts Laban, his duplicitous father-in-law, who defends his actions by (you guessed it) appealing to primogeniture. "It is not our custom here to give the younger daughter in marriage before the older one."[12] Jacob will not be denied and wastes no time in negotiating a second marriage to Rachel. Those same patriarchal conventions should have entitled Leah to the honor and rights of senior wife and her firstborn son, Reuben, to the double portion and Jacob's patriarchal blessing. None of that was to be.

The fierce rivalry between the two sisters in the race to produce the most sons for Jacob set the stage for Leah's sons to suffer the father wound, for their mother was "unloved." The naming of her sons reads like an angst-ridden page from Leah's tear stained private journal: Reuben, for "It is because the LORD has seen my misery. Surely my husband will love me now"; Simeon, "Because the LORD heard that I am not loved"; Levi, "Now at last my husband will become attached to me, because I have borne him three sons"; Judah, "This time I will praise the LORD"; Issachar, "God has rewarded me for giving my maidservant to my husband" (How easy to be blinded by our own pain and simultaneously indifferent to pain we inflict on someone else); and Zebulun, "This time my husband will treat me with honor because I have borne him six sons."[13]

Sadly, not even birthing six sons could win Jacob over. Even Leah's six sons combined could not compete with the place in Jacob's heart reserved for Rachel's firstborn son, Joseph. According to Jacob's calculus, one is greater than six.

Like Julian Lennon, Judah sees his mother displaced by his father's love for another woman. We aren't told when it dawned on Judah that his mother "was not loved."[14] If he didn't catch on before Rachel gave birth to Joseph, it took on glaring and devastating dimensions afterwards.

Judah was at least in his teens when his father braced to reunite with his estranged brother Esau, whose last heard words regarding Jacob were threats of murder. Word came that Esau was heading toward Jacob with four hundred men. Terrified and fearing the worst, Jacob arranged his company into two groups, putting servants first and family last, with Rachel and Joseph bringing up the rear—a physical statement revealing that Rachel and Joseph are Jacob's treasures and the ones he feared losing the most. Even a young child would realize his father was using him, his mother, and her children as human shields to protect his beloved Rachel and Joseph.

If the reader doesn't pick up on this, the narrator makes it plain: Jacob "loved Joseph *more than any of his other sons*" and made his preference public by making Joseph "a richly orna-mented robe."[15] This robe was more than a colorful garment; it was symbol of royalty and preeminence. "By this regal apparel Jacob publicly designates Joseph as the ruler over the family. Jacob wants to pass on the rule to godly Joseph."[16]

Instead of smoothing over the injured feelings this under-standably provoked, Joseph inflames his older half-brothers' indignation by parading around in his royal robe and ratting on them to their father. Adding insult to injury, Joseph cavalierly describes two dreams he had where the whole family bows down to him. Even their father is taken aback. But Judah and his brothers have had their fill. Their simmering jealousy becomes "an escalating hatred,"[17] as murderous thoughts take root.

RIVALRY REDUX

Jacob's older sons are miles from home grazing their father's flocks when Joseph appears in the distance. They see a fortuitous opportunity to rid themselves of "that dreamer" and begin plotting murder. Reuben, the eldest, prevents the violence with an alternate plan that stops short of shedding blood by abandoning Joseph to die a slow death in a cistern,[18] where Joseph—stripped of his robe—is promptly deposited. Reuben planned to circle back later to pull Joseph out. After Reuben leaves, a caravan of Ishmaelites en route to Egypt shows up, and a new plan comes together.

Now Judah takes charge as the coldly calculating instigator of a ruthless plan to sell Joseph as a slave. The brothers become human traffickers. Over the pleading cries of the seventeen-year-old Joseph, money changes hands. Joseph is bound and carted off into the living death of slavery and sold in Egypt to Potiphar, captain of Pharaoh's guard.

Meanwhile, there is a cover-up. The brothers take Joseph's royal robe dipped in goat's blood to deceive their father. They merely show the robe to their father and "let the contrived object ... do their lying for them."[19] Jacob himself pronounces Joseph dead and the cause of death a wild beast.

Their father Jacob is inconsolable. Readers—in the grips of a page-turner and eager to learn what becomes of Joseph—are completely irritated by what comes next. Instead of following the action and Joseph into Egypt, the narrator takes a detour and goes with Judah, who becomes the central figure in the story. The shift in the story may annoy readers and create problems for preachers because it's difficult to find anything

redeeming to preach from this R-rated story involving prostitution. But the Judah story, which seems wholly unrelated to the
central plot, is utterly pivotal to how the Joseph story finally
turns out. "Without this account of Tamar putting her father-in-
law to shame, we should be hard pressed to explain the change
in [Judah's] character."[20]

Kidnapping and selling his brother into slavery are just the
beginning of Judah's descent into the malestrom. In *Falling
Upward*, Richard Rohr writes what could easily be a synopsis
of Judah's story.

> The bottom line of the Gospel is that most of us have to hit
> some kind of bottom before we even start the real spiritual
> journey.... God knows that all of us will fall somehow. Those
> events that lead us to "catastrophize" out of all proportion
> must be business as usual for God — at least six billion times
> a day.... Failure and suffering are the great equalizers and
> levelers among humans. Success is just the opposite.... The
> genius of the Gospel was that it included the problem inside
> the solution. The falling became the standing. The stumbling
> became the finding. The dying became the rising.[21]

Judah is about to "catastrophize." The malestrom has him in
its grasp and will drag him into the darkest depths. But Judah
will rise again too, although not until he breaks free of the father
wound's hold on him.

The narrative juxtaposes Joseph and Judah. They are polar
opposites — the proverbial white sheep and black sheep of the
family. All that Joseph is, Judah is not. The two brothers face off
at the cistern where Joseph is outnumbered and Judah sells him
as a slave. They meet again in Egypt where family power dynamics are reversed. All eleven brothers cower before an empowered
Joseph they do not recognize, and Judah steps forward as the
family leader once again, this time when Benjamin — the youngest of the twelve, Joseph's only full brother, and Jacob's new
favorite son — is threatened with slavery.

Judah's sudden ascendancy to leadership among his brothers may be the result of primogeniture. Up to this point in the narrative, all three of Judah's older brothers (Jacob's first three sons) have discredited themselves and fallen out of favor with their father. Instead of bringing honor to Jacob (as worthy sons do), they disgrace him by their odious conduct.

Reuben, Jacob's eldest, sleeps with his father's concubine Bilhah — a defiant act by which a son becomes "a stench in [his] father's nostrils."[22] After the rape of their sister Dinah, Simeon and Levi (sons two and three) seek to vindicate family honor with a bloody massacre of the Shechemites, making Jacob himself "a stench"[23] and raising the threat of retaliation from more powerful neighbors. But instead of crowning Judah as the logical and culturally legitimate next in line, Jacob bypasses him and six other sons to shower affection and firstborn honors on Joseph.

Judah's father wound sends him spiraling into the malestrom. He drifts away from his family into Canaanite territory, which represents more than a change in geography. He puts down roots with the Canaanites, forges alliances with Canaanites, marries a Canaanite woman, and ultimately behaves like one of them. Instead of raising sons to walk before Yahweh faithfully, two of his three sons are described as "wicked in the LORD's sight" and lose their lives on that account.[24]

It is worth noting that the narrator makes no mention of Jacob being distraught over Judah's disappearance, of frantic attempts to track down and locate his second missing son, or of Judah's father scanning the horizon every day in search of his returning prodigal. Jacob's silence is an awful contrast with his inconsolable grief over Joseph.

Judah's father wound is real. It cuts deep and travels with him into the final chapter.

But Judah is Yahweh's son too and the object of Yahweh's love. And although Judah doesn't know it yet, Yahweh is orchestrating an intervention through Judah's Canaanite daughter-in-law, Tamar. She becomes the means by whom God reaches into the malestrom and rescues Judah.

PATRIARCHY DIMINISHES THE *EZER KENEGDO*

Judah's story puts on full display the destructive powers of patriarchy against men with an appalling trail of suffering and wreckage that leads back to the patriarch Abraham. This fallen social system lowers men's sights and aspirations to a horizontal competitive quest for male power to win and achieve preeminence over other men. It distracts them from the loftier calling and the greater dignity of imaging God and walking faithfully before him. Patriarchy withholds from men the freedom and flourishing that God envisions for his sons.

But patriarchy comes at a huge cost for both genders. By elevating men over women, patriarchy marginalizes females and prevents them from thriving as the *ezer kenegdo* warriors God created them to be and that God's sons need.

Jacob had two wives and two concubines, but not one of them reaches that *ezer kenegdo* level of involvement in his story. Under patriarchy, women are valued for their physical beauty, the pleasure they provide for men, and/or their ability to produce sons for their husband. It deprives them of agency and voice. The culture views them this way and that's how they most often view themselves.

Jacob's two wives are locked into this mindset. Neither seems to engage, much less challenge, Jacob at the deepest level where he would most benefit from an *ezer*. It is far worse for Jacob's concubines Bilhah and Zilpah. These slave girls have no say when their job description expands to include sex with Jacob to produce more sons for the warring sisters, Leah and Rachel. We can dress up the story all we like to make it suitable for children's Sunday School lessons and proper sermons. But horrific things are going on behind the scenes. Once again we see the ugly face of sexual exploitation in this story. Sadly, some things never change.

Judah may be incensed by his mother's misery, but his story can hardly be considered an improvement on his father's views of women. But unlike Jacob, Judah will encounter an *ezer-warrior* in his story.

THE RIGHTEOUS PROSTITUTE

Tamar enters the story within the confines of traditional patriarchy and as an outsider to God's covenant with Abraham. But she will not remain there long. At first, she, like other women, assumes a passive role. She is married off to Er, Judah's firstborn. When Er dies without a male heir, Judah marries her to his second son, Onan. According to patriarchal customs widely practiced at the time (later formalized as the Levirate Law under Moses),[25] the surviving brother and the deceased man's widow are honor bound to marry and produce the missing male heir who will assume the vacant spot on the family tree.

Onan faces a terrible dilemma. Crassly stated, the death of his older brother means a sudden lucrative jump in his inheritance. Now, possessing the rights of the firstborn—including the double portion—Onan's inheritance skyrockets from a modest one-fourth to a whopping two-thirds. However, if Tamar bears a son, Onan's share shrinks back down to one fourth. You can just see Onan poring over the numbers.

For Onan, success with Tamar in replacing his dead brother with a baby boy represents a dramatic cut in pay he is unwilling to take. So he fakes family honor by marrying Tamar, using her for his pleasure, but withdrawing and spilling his seed on the ground to prevent her from conceiving. In a patriarchal culture, such behavior dishonored not only Tamar, but his dead brother, and family honor. It cost him his life.

Now, with only one surviving son, Judah links Tamar to his losses and will not risk marrying Shelah to Tamar. So he sends her packing back to her father's house with promises he doesn't intend to keep. Returning to her father's home to live as an unmarried daughter is a deep disgrace for Tamar. Time passes. Shelah reaches marriageable age, and Tamar realizes Judah's promises are empty.

Ironically, despite patriarchy's marginalization of women, it provides the motive that mobilizes Tamar to become the true hero of the story. *Patriarchal concepts of family honor and duty to her dead husband drive her.* If we miss this one piece of the puzzle, we'll unjustly reduce her motives to desperate longings for a baby or a chance to get even with her lying father-in-law.

Tamar may have been within her legal rights. Based on ancient Hittite and Assyrian laws that regulated levirate duty, marriage of the father-in-law to his son's widow was a legal option if no brother fulfilled this family duty. Still, Tamar is taking an enormous chance—actually risking her life as it turns out—to provide a son for her dead husband.

To get the true heart-stopping danger of her actions, picture this story taking place in today's Middle East. What would happen to an unmarried woman who prostituted herself and got pregnant?

The short version is this: Tamar learns that Judah, emerging from grief over his wife's death, is on his way to the sheep shearing—a festive event with plenty of food and drink. She plots to exploit his loneliness by posing as a prostitute.

She stations herself in Judah's path. Her shrewd plan reveals remarkable insight into Judah's character. Who would believe Judah would solicit the services of a prostitute? But he does and adds "john"[26] to his personal resume. The contrast with Joseph is vivid, for in Egypt lonely Joseph is fleeing the seductions of Potiphar's wife.

Tamar drives a hard bargain with Judah. The deed is done, and she walks away with Judah's seal and staff as a pledge of payment—the equivalent today of his credit card and driver's license—evidence she will produce to establish Judah's paternity.

When Judah learns Tamar is pregnant from prostitution, with blinding speed and shocking hypocrisy he orders her to be publicly burned to death. It is a frightening display of his patriarchal power over Tamar. She is instantly in peril of one of the world's worst atrocities: honor killings. The horror of this moment must not be minimized in any sense. Every day, countless young women are tortured and killed for "violating family honor"—however the powers that be may define it. It can even be a punishment for a girl who is raped.

But instead of suffering an honor killing, Tamar publicly confronts Judah himself. Her outrageous courage brings a sudden end to Judah's descent into the malestrom, as she shines the light of truth on Judah. This is the moment the prodigal comes to his senses.

Negative opinions of Tamar may persist—but these are not based on the text. Her interactions with Judah and the twins she births to replace his two deceased (and undeserving) sons, rank her as one of the brightest lights (despite her Canaanite origins) in Israel's constellation of female matriarchs.[27] Judah is the first to place her there when he says, "She is righteous; I am not."[28]

FALLING UPWARD

The full impact of Judah's encounter with Tamar doesn't come to light until a chastened Judah and his half-brother Joseph come face to face in Egypt a second time during a devastating famine. This time the tables have turned. Joseph, who has surged in power and is now second in command only to Pharaoh, holds absolute power over his brothers who have come to purchase food from him. The brothers do not recognize the young boy they sold as a slave. Against their father's fears and protests, they have brought Jacob's youngest son, Benjamin, Joseph's only full brother and Jacob's new favorite son. During an earlier encounter, Joseph demanded they bring their youngest brother and said they would not see his face again if they came without him.

A crisis ensues when Joseph's silver cup is discovered in Benjamin's sack, and Joseph threatens to enslave him. The same brothers who ignored his cries and sold him into slavery some twenty years earlier are now at the mercy of Joseph.

Judah commands the spotlight and leads us to the missing chapter. With a throbbing *unhealed* father wound, without realizing he is speaking to Joseph, the brother he once wanted to kill and trafficked as a slave, and with his father still playing favorites, Judah makes one of the most moving speeches in all of Scripture.

> "Please, my lord, let your servant say just one word to you. Please, do not be angry with me, even though you are as powerful as Pharaoh himself.
>
> "My lord, previously you asked us, your servants, 'Do you have a father or a brother?' And we responded, 'Yes, my lord, we have a father who is an old man, and his youngest son is a child of his old age. His full brother is dead, and he alone is left of his mother's children, *and his father loves him very much.'*
>
> "And you said to us, 'Bring him here so I can see him with my own eyes.' But we said to you, 'My lord, the boy cannot leave his father, for his father would die.' But you told us, 'Unless your youngest brother comes with you, you will never see my face again.'
>
> " ... Later, when [our father] said, 'Go back again and buy us more food,' we replied, 'We can't go unless you let our youngest brother go with us. We'll never get to see the man's face unless our youngest brother is with us.'

"Then my father said to us, 'As you know, my wife had two sons, and one of them went away and never returned. Doubtless he was torn to pieces by some wild animal. I have never seen him since. Now if you take his brother away from me, and any harm comes to him, you will send this grieving, white-haired man to his grave.'

"And now, my lord, I cannot go back to my father without the boy. Our father's life is bound up in the boy's life. If he sees that the boy is not with us, our father will die. We, your servants, will indeed be responsible for sending that grieving, white-haired man to his grave.

"My lord, I guaranteed to my father that I would take care of the boy. I told him, 'If I don't bring him back to you, I will bear the blame forever.' So please, my lord, *let me stay here as a slave instead of the boy*, and let the boy return with his brothers. For how can I return to my father if the boy is not with me? *I couldn't bear to see the anguish this would cause my father!*"[29]

Judah pleads for Benjamin's freedom with the passion of a prodigal who is utterly redeemed and transformed. He freely describes Benjamin as the son his father "loves"[30]—a remarkable acceptance of "the painful fact of paternal favoritism ('and his father loves him') that was the root of the brothers' hostility to Joseph."[31] He recounts his father saying, *"Two did my wife bear me,"*[32] as though Judah, his mother Leah, and nine of Jacob's sons never existed.

One cannot but marvel as Robert Alter does: "Judah appears now to accept this outrageous favoritism as part of what his father is, part of the father he must still love."[33] Against the pain of his father wound, Judah voices his heart's desire to spare his father the "misery" that losing this second son will cause. Then, in a staggering act of self-sacrifice—Judah offers himself as a slave in place of his father's favorite son Benjamin.

A person would have to be made of stone to witness this moment dry-eyed.

The Judah who stands before Joseph and pleads for Benjamin is not the same Judah who once callously sold his brother into slavery. Judah's father wound remains, but it has lost its power over him. His father is still playing favorites and will continue when he is finally reunited with his long-lost beloved son Joseph. Leah and her sons will remain in the shadows. Patriarchy is still entrenched, but the malestrom's power over Judah has been dismantled. Sacrificing himself as a slave in place of his father's darling Benjamin is perhaps the freest choice Judah has ever made. For the first time in his life, he is walking before God faithfully and being blameless. A very different selfless "not of this world" brand of manhood emerges.

Judah doesn't rise to power in the world's eyes. He remains in the brokenness that none of God's sons can escape. He will never enjoy the love his father lavishes on his youngest brothers. His father wound won't go away. Judah's painful circumstances remain unchanged, but Judah is not the same. He is an utterly changed man—the kind of man who has reconnected with the Center and now seeks the kingdom of God. Judah embodies the radical, self-sacrificing way of Jesus that is "not of this world" and gives us a startling glimpse of that missing chapter. So does the man in the next chapter, who defies patriarchal gender stereotypes and all of his critics by forging strong kingdom alliances with women.

DISCUSSION QUESTIONS

1. From your own story, how have your father's words (positive or negative or missing altogether) had enormous sticking power with you?

2. Why do you think Judah's father wound drove him into a spiritual nosedive?

3. Why did Tamar's confrontation with Judah prove to be a mercy and a turning point for him?

4. Do you agree with Richard Rohr that the father wound is "so deep and so all-pervasive in so many parts of the world that its healing could well be the most radical social reform conceivable"? Why or why not?

5. How did Judah battle the malestrom, and what does his story teach us about God's calling on his sons?

CHAPTER 4

THE RISE OF WOMEN

It was an "unforeseen situation."

AN "UNFORESEEN SITUATION" (indeed, an unimaginable situation) occurred on June 7, 1890, when a young woman at Cambridge University *bested* the male students in the mathematical examinations by thirteen points. These examinations were designed to challenge the finest minds the British Empire could produce. It was "the first and only time a woman ranked first in the mathematical examinations held at the University of Cambridge."[1] Philippa Fawcett's academic prowess shook the prejudices of the Victorian age. But it would never happen again, for shortly afterward the exams were discontinued.

Fast forward to the twenty-first century and what was universally regarded as an "unforeseen situation" in Victorian England is an everyday occurrence. Today's world is awash in "unforeseen situations" involving smart, high-achieving, successful women. In her ominously subtitled book, *Manning Up: How the Rise of Women Has Turned Men into Boys*, Kay S. Hymowitz observes:

> For the first time ever, and I do mean ever, young women are reaching their twenties with more achievements, more education, more property, and arguably, more ambition than their male counterparts. Throughout human existence, men were the ones holding the jobs, the degrees, the money, the power, the independence, and the expectation for action on

the public stage. Now men have met their match—in many respects, their superiors.[2]

In American academic institutions, "Women earn almost 60 percent of all bachelors degrees ... 60 percent of masters degrees, about half of all law and medical degrees, and about 44 percent of all business degrees."[3] In many cases, they are outperforming male students who, for the first time, must compete with women for privileges and priority. Economist Claudia Goldin labeled the transformation that has taken place in the workplace the "Quiet Revolution," as more and more women take their place in the marketplace and function at home as joint decision makers with their spouses. Today's empty nest has been reenvisioned as a launching pad as women pick up where they left off to pursue their education and careers.

Women have headed up significant organizations like the US Secret Service and the Securities and Exchange Commission. Half of Ivy League schools have had female presidents at the helm, as have major corporations such as IBM, General Motors, Lockheed Martin, and the *New York Times*. For the first time in the history of our nation (as of 2015), three women sit on the US Supreme Court, and more than one female politician has her eye on the White House.

This seismic cultural shift is by no means restricted to the United States. Elsewhere female heads of state are not just a matter of wishful thinking. Germany, Ireland, South Korea, Brazil, Costa Rica, India, Bangladesh, Croatia, Slovakia, New Zealand, and Iceland are only a few of the countries that have already crossed that gender line.

In recent years women have defied patriarchal odds in nonwestern countries in dramatic ways that would have made Philippa Fawcett proud. In 2003 a brutal civil war was tearing Liberia apart, when thousands of "ordinary" Liberian mothers, grandmothers, aunts, and daughters armed only with fierce resolve overcame powerful warlords and the country's ruthless dictator, Charles Taylor. When peace talks stalled, these women barricaded themselves in a government building, stubbornly refusing to leave until a peace agreement was reached. Their valiant efforts not only brought peace but also Africa's first female head of state, Ellen Johnson Sirleaf.[4]

Then there is the irrepressible Malala Yousafzai, the fifteen-year-old Pakistani schoolgirl. Even a Taliban gunman's bullet to the head could not stop her advocacy for girls' education in Pakistan. Instead of silencing her forever, the Taliban gave her a global platform. On her sixteenth birthday in 2013, after an arduous but determined recovery, she stood — poised and unbending — before the United Nations General Assembly to reiterate her renewed commitment to education for girls. In 2014 she was awarded the Nobel Peace Prize (shared with Kailash Satyarthi, the Hindu children's rights activist from India).

Tom Brokaw, one of America's most esteemed newsmen and father of three high-achieving daughters, predicted the twenty-first century will become known as "the Century of Women."[5]

Blame it on feminism, contraception, affirmative action, access to higher education, postmodernism, economic changes, exploding technology, the Internet, or global warming, but make no mistake about it — the world has changed. Even in cultures where advances for women are lagging and the disparity between the sexes leaves women at an appalling disadvantage, women continue to defy the odds by creating "unforeseen situations" of the most improbable sort.

SHIFTING GENDER ROLES IN THE CHURCH

The church is not immune to this tidal wave of change. Today's churches are filled with successful Christian women who are climbing the corporate ladder and occupying leadership positions in a wide range of professions. More and more women are in the workplace by choice and calling—not out of necessity. Evangelical seminaries are producing gifted female graduates, and many are moving into all sorts of ministry and pastoral leadership positions. In this age of the Internet, some evangelical female bloggers have followings that surpass megachurch attendance. Young girls have ambitions and dreams that are different than those of their parents. Those dreams may include marriage and children, but they have other dreams as well.

Plenty of Christian men welcome these changes and in fact have advocated for them. But others view the rise of women with concern, even alarm, and strive to stem the tide. The belief in a zero-sum game between the genders, where gains for women represent losses for men, makes the rise of women difficult to swallow. Women once lauded as "the backbone of the church" are now perceived as a threat.

This is not a new situation. The Bible contains plenty of "unforeseen situations" where women appear to outshine the men. These stories create enormous problems for interpreters because they violate the patriarchal principle that men lead and women follow. The power of these biblical narratives is intensified by the fact that these stories aren't situated in an egalitarian western culture, but are embedded in a full-blown patriarchal context where men are primary and hold the reins of power.

DIMINISHING BARAK

The classic "unforeseen situation" in the Bible is the Old Testament story of Deborah, Barak, and the mallet-wielding female, Jael, who drove a tent peg through the head of Israel's sleeping enemy, General Sisera. The story is a gender minefield for those who seek to regulate the cultural rise of women. In this Old Testament narrative, women are the heroes, while the men (primarily Barak) draw a firestorm of criticism for being cowardly, spineless, and weak. Not only is the leading male figure in this story bested by a woman—Barak is *bested by two women*!

Debating gender camps are quick to take sides. Egalitarians view Deborah as one more biblical nail in patriarchy's coffin. African scholar Tokunboh Adeyemo, who was born and bred in a thoroughly patriarchal culture, could not resist pointing out the countercultural implications of Deborah's leadership role in this biblical story. "Despite living in a male-dominated culture, she served as head of state, commander-in-chief and chief justice.[6] Her achievement should put an end to debate about whether women can provide leadership."[7] For many women searching the Bible for confirmation of their God-given leadership gifts and calling, Deborah is their "*Aha!*" moment. "If Deborah, why not me?!"

Complementarians respond to the Deborah story by scaling down her significance and caricaturing her leadership as nothing more than a punishment for men—"a living indictment of the weakness of Barak and other men in Israel who should have been more courageous leaders."[8] They warn against drawing conclusions about female leadership from her story and argue that modern Christians ought not to make theological deductions from the "precarious" period of the judges.[9] The inference is that Deborah would never have risen to power if men had been leading as God intends. Deborah, they insist, is an exception to the rule and "a special case."[10] Some complementarians even go so far as to reduce her prophetic role "to private and individual instruction"[11]—despite the fact that she publicly calls the nation to war and publicly accompanies the general and his army into battle.

Egalitarians, even as they exalt the leadership role of Deborah, have little respect for Barak. Echoing the complementarians, they depict Barak as a "spineless" man who reacts to God's call to battle with "childlike overdependence on Deborah and implied lack of trust in God."[12] These egalitarians conclude it was Barak's failure as a leader that "forced women [Deborah] to step across contemporary Israelite boundaries and fulfill the divine purpose."[13] Ironically, both sides of the gender debate make the "weakness" of Barak the proximate cause of Deborah's irregular elevation. Modern patriarchal assumptions create strange bedfellows.

All too often, Barak becomes the red-faced poster-child of cowardice, the icon of diminished manhood, a casualty of patriarchal standards of what it means to be a man. The entire narrative becomes a potent opportunity for chastising men for failing to man up.

As we might expect, the criticism doesn't stop with Barak, but extends to Deborah and Jael, despite their being hailed as the obvious heroes of the story. Deborah is demeaned as nothing more than "punishment" for fainthearted men. She is an exception to patriarchal norms and so her leadership doesn't carry any lasting significance. Once I even heard Deborah criticized for singing too much about herself, although I've never heard anyone lodge that same criticism at King David. Consistency is not always a virtue in the gender debates.

Jael, in turn, is disparaged as "treacherous" and "subversive to her husband," and is even lampooned for violating ancient customs of hospitality. Some speculate that she sexually enticed Sisera into her tent. Her actions are interpreted as "deviant" for undermining the proper role of a wife.[14] In other words, Jael was unsubmissive to her husband.

THE HOLY TRIUMVIRATE OF TWO WOMEN AND A MAN

Something is terribly out of whack here. The biblical narrative contains not the slightest whisper of criticism for any of the three leading characters. Not a murmur! Not here or anywhere else in Scripture. To the contrary, this triumvirate of two women and a man are honored and praised to the heights. Critics, it seems, have gotten caught up in the contemporary gender debate and lost sight of the Bible in the process.

The Bible doesn't caricature Deborah as a "fallback" for failed male leadership. The fact that she appears at the beginning of Judges situates her as one of the strongest and best of Israel's judges (it is generally recognized that as the book of Judges progresses, the quality and character of Israel's judges decline precipitously). Her deep theological words are memorialized in the Song of Deborah.[15] According to traditional interpretations, Deborah, like Moses, judged disputes among tribal elders.[16] Like Samuel, she combined the twin callings of judge and prophet. Some contrast her with the other judges who were military deliverers, a description that is never used for Deborah. However, Deborah didn't shrink from military conflict, but accompanied Barak and his army into battle.

The Bible never portrays Jael as treacherous or committing a morally unjustified act of murder either. It may very well be that she was insubordinate to her husband, Heber, but considering Israel's decisive defeat of the Canaanites, Jael's actions may have saved her husband's life. The text informs us that Heber was a traitor enjoying "friendly terms"[17] with Israel's Canaanite oppressor, King Jabin. Jael's first loyalty it appears was to Israel—who can criticize that? Based on what the narrator actually says about Jael, such criticisms of Jael are, in the words of Bruce Waltke, "arbitrary interpretations."[18] Instead, Jael is celebrated as "most blessed of women,"[19] high praise indeed that sounds a lot like the similarly blessed virgin Mary.

As for Barak, Scripture nowhere intimates that Barak is a wimp, a coward, or weak in faith. In fact the opposite is declared—and this surely *must* be factored into how we view the so-called weak-willed general of little faith. Barak's name is emblazoned in the Bible's Hall of Fame. Hebrews 11 heralds Barak as *a champion of faith* along with the likes of "Gideon,

Samson, Jephthah, David, Samuel and the prophets" (which includes Deborah), "who through faith conquered kingdoms, administered justice, and gained what was promised; who ... escaped the edge of the sword; whose weakness was turned to strength; and who became powerful in battle and routed foreign armies."[20]

Reading the story, it is difficult to avoid Deborah's heroic leadership over Israel, Barak's valor in battle, and Jael's courageous tent-peg termination of General Sisera—unless, of course, one comes to the biblical text with a prior agenda. Together these three are Israel's praiseworthy deliverers—a "death-defying 'triumvirate' who cooperate to effect deliverance."[21]

SISERA'S HOBNAILED JACKBOOT

The context for the pivotal battle is that Israel has suffered *twenty long years* of "cruel" Canaanite oppression under the hobnailed jackboot of the pitiless Sisera. (My mind inevitably connects to circumstances in today's Middle East as ISIS gains control of Iraqi and Syrian territory.) Things were so bad in Israel that the people no longer traveled on the open roads but for safety's sake made their way "through thickets and rough mountain passes to avoid detection by the enemy ... farmers refused to go out to the fields, and trade among the tribes of Israel came to a standstill."[22] Much like the notorious Thirty Years' War that paralyzed Central Europe between 1618–1648, Sisera's tyranny brought suffering at every level—from poverty, to violence, to sexual exploitation. Those of us who have always enjoyed prosperity, safety, and freedom (blessings that even in the West aren't shared or enjoyed by all) are in no position to judge Barak's actions when we know nothing first-hand of such horrific circumstances. Nigerian theologian Tokunboh Adeyemo reminds Westerners that people like those "who live in wartorn regions of Africa will recognize the types of disruption of normal life that is described."[23] We in the West can only wonder at the terrifying realities that lie behind his words.

After twenty years of Sisera's suppression, the Israelites cry out to Yahweh for mercy. And Yahweh hears.

WHAT REALLY HAPPENED

Throughout the pages of the Old Testament, God's people cry out to him for deliverance from one calamity or another. Typical are the words of David in Psalm 34: "The righteous cry out, and the LORD hears them; he delivers them from all their troubles. The LORD is close to the brokenhearted and saves those who are crushed in spirit."[24] These same words might very well have been uttered by the Israelites suffering under Sisera.

In biblical times, God usually answered by raising up a male. Explanations that God raised up a woman because the men were weak and failing to lead don't hold up. God's story includes plenty of situations when Israel needed strong leadership, and God called on men who weren't archetypical leaders and who often resisted God's call and exhibited fear: a coward (like Gideon), the insecure (like Moses or Jeremiah), or a teenager (like David or Daniel).

This time God raises up a female, and her resume is impressive. Deborah is a true prophetess. God speaks through her to his people. She is a judge in Israel, described as "leading Israel at that time."[25] Deborah is the nation's undisputed leader, and the people turn to her for judgments. An interpretation that is more consistent with what is actually happening in the context is that the oppressed Israelites who are crying out to the Lord for help[26] appeal to Deborah, Israel's leader and God's prophet for *justice* [mišpāṭ] or "for *the* judgment" (emphasis original).[27] In other words, they are looking to her as God's prophet for a *particular* judgment—to deliver Israel from Sisera. They want her to act. This appeal is followed by Deborah's first recorded act as Israel's commander-in-chief: she summons "Barak son of Abinoam from Kedesh"[28] to battle against the enemy, mapping out strategy, promising victory, and claiming Yahweh's authority for her command.

Barak must assemble ten thousand men from the tribes of Naphtali and Zebulun and lead them to Mount Tabor—some 1,843 feet above sea level.[29] Yahweh will then lure Sisera and his army of nine hundred iron chariots into the dry Kishon River bed below and hand Sisera and his minions over to Barak in defeat. After twenty years of oppression, so we read, at last victory is just around the corner.

But instead of saluting his commander-in-chief and giving a Braveheart war cry, like William Wallace at the Battle of Stirling Bridge (1297), Barak hesitates (hence the charge of cowardice). He actually refuses to go into battle *unless* Deborah goes too. In stark contrast, Deborah has the *chutzpa* to respond with an unflinching, "I will go."

But the prophetess has more to say. She prophesies that the ultimate honor for the promised victory over Sisera will go to a woman—at this point most assume Deborah herself.[30]

According to traditional gendered interpretations, both Sisera and Barak suffer the ultimate indignity of being outdone by a female. This makes sense in the case of Sisera, whose memory will be permanently blemished by the epithet, more feared than death itself: "A woman killed him."[31]

Understanding Barak is more complicated and more nuanced. From a patriarchal perspective, Barak too fails. It is argued that because his immediate response to Deborah's charge is considered unmanly, Deborah is issuing the divine punishment that Barak forfeits the honor of administering the *coup de grâce* ("finishing blow") to Sisera. We need to pause the action for a moment to explore a different, nonpatriarchal interpretation of this story.

Imagine being in General Barak's sandals. These are the

realities he faces: Sisera is armed to the teeth with nine hundred chariots of iron — the latest in military hardware. These iron chariots give Sisera an "unassailable superiority on the low, flat land of the coastal plain and the broad Jezreel Valley."[32] And what of Barak's army? In contrast to Sisera's professional heavily-armed forces, Barak has a rag-tag army of Israelite peasants, inexperienced volunteers who are virtually unarmed, for the text informs us that "not a shield or spear was seen among forty thousand in Israel."[33]

Barak is walking into a military disaster, unless God miraculously intervenes. Although we aren't told that Barak was afraid, a little fear in the heart of a general is probably a good thing when the prospect of war is looming. The burning issue for Barak isn't, "Why is a woman telling me what to do?" or "I don't feel safe without Deborah." The really important issue for him is one that matters to us all: "Is Yahweh in the battle with me or not?" This is the tipping point for Barak and a profound issue of faith. The odds are ridiculously stacked against Israel, and too many lives are at stake. Israel has gone twenty long years without relief from Yahweh. Barak can't afford a mistake. He wants to know if this is Yahweh's battle. If Deborah's word is false, this mission is suicidal.

Jesus says a lot of things that are hard to understand. But this statement seems pretty straightforward and may explain Barak's reluctance: "Suppose a king is about to go to war against another king. Will he not first sit down and consider *whether he is able with ten thousand men* to oppose the one coming against him with twenty thousand? If he is not able, he will send a delegation while the other is still a long way off and will ask for terms of peace."[34]

Barak exhibits the kind of caution any credible general must possess. So he asks Yahweh's prophet to back her words with action. "If you go with me, I will go; but if you don't go with me, I won't go." This is not a gender issue, although Barak is well aware that this prophet is a female. The terms he sets focus on her prophetic role. Barak wants confirmation that the prophet is really relaying the commands of Yahweh. Some even think "Barak treats Deborah as other Israelite combatants elsewhere treat the Ark [of the Covenant], the symbol of God's presence and power"[35] when he insists that she go too.

Deborah doesn't blink. She will go. Her answer confirms that the prophet is indeed revealing the word of the Lord. Her words to Barak remind me of Elijah's rather peculiar test to demonstrate the superiority of Yahweh. Elijah pours twelve barrels of water on the altar while asking Yahweh to set it on fire. As unlikely as it was for any fire to light up that water-soaked altar (which Yahweh does)[36] so here, Yahweh will not allow the defeat of Sisera to be seen as a military victory. It is Yahweh's victory, and he will prove this by ending Sisera's life—the man all Israel fears—at the hands of a noncombatant woman, in this case, Jael.

The words of Deborah are not intended to shame Barak, but to demonstrate that Yahweh is the true victor. When the battle is over, far from being threatened by Judge Deborah's authority or crestfallen when Jael takes the glory for killing Sisera, Barak will be worshiping Yahweh and singing the praises of both women.[37] Indeed, Barak is overjoyed that God raised up two *ezer*-warriors to secure the victory.

TENT PEG TERMINATION

With the prophet Deborah at his side, Barak leads his peasant army against the dreaded Canaanite General Sisera. The battle is joined at the Kishon River, not far from the camp of Heber the Kenite, Jael's husband. As it turns out, someone from Heber's camp (possibly Heber himself) provides intelligence to King Jabin about the movements of Barak and his troops that prepare Sisera and his forces for battle.

Barak's army had taken up positions on Mount Tabor and thus had the benefit of high ground. Sisera's iron chariots roll toward the usually dry riverbed of the Kishon River, expecting to have full maneuverability and thus the military advantage. It seems that Yahweh sent a heavy downpour of rain, the dry Kishon River became a torrent, and the heavy iron chariots got stuck in the mire. Barak's peasant army then launched their attack with devastating effect. With his own chariot bogged down in the mud, Sisera flees on foot.[38]

The defeated general arrives at Heber's camp, believing he has found refuge among friends. But Sisera's arrival places Jael in a precarious situation. On the one hand, harboring the oppressor of Israel would land Jael and her husband in a heap of trouble. On the other hand, she's already in trouble with this dangerous and desperate fugitive in her tent.[39] What is Jael to do?

Sisera's arrival might be likened to the six-foot-six-inch Saudi terrorist Osama bin Laden showing up on your doorstep expecting safe haven. Jael will not run for cover or wring her hands waiting for Heber to tell her what to do. Nor does she stop to question the appropriateness of a woman doing anything beyond lowering her eyes and submissively doing whatever the mighty Sisera requires. Jael decides to take matters into her own hands—literally.

I'm completely flummoxed when modern interpreters accuse Jael of violating patriarchal traditions. Statements like this are hard to fathom when a known killer is inside your tent: "Not only had she broken fundamental social rules of wifely support; she had also violated deeply entrenched customs of ancient Near Eastern hospitality. First she, a woman, usurps his exclusive right as a male to offer hospitality to a male. Then, having lulled her guest into a false sense of security, she premeditates and executes his murder."[40]

Clearly the point of this story is *not* about Near Eastern customs of hospitality or cultural rules of wifely obedience. This is to read this biblical episode through a gendered lens. In fact, this dramatic story is about much more than gender roles and customs. Jael may very well be saving Heber's traitorous neck, but the story points the reader in a more theocentric direction.

GOD IN THE MARGINS

One of the inevitable consequences of reading the Bible through a gendered lens is that God is shoved to the margins. He is reduced to a sidebar: issuing orders via Deborah and showing up on cue to deliver the needed miracle—opening the rain clouds, turning the Kishon River into a deluge, and clogging the wheels of the chariots. But this is the malestrom at work—removing God from the center and causing us to focus on gender issues and to miss the main point of the Bible, including the main point of this story, which is to reveal God to us.

We are witnessing a powerful David and Goliath story. The narrative does not demean or scold men as wimps or diminish women as second-string quarterbacks. Rather, it contains the hope-filled promise that God hears the cries of the oppressed (as his true image bearers also should hear) and assures us that the darkness will not ultimately prevail. The story shines a light on even darker evils of the malestrom and the lows to which men sink when they rule over, dominate, crush, and oppress other people as Sisera does.

The fight against Sisera and his iron chariots is one more local manifestation of the larger global battle for God's kingdom. The central issue in this story is not gender roles or male versus female but an issue we face every day in the battles God is calling us to fight. Can we trust God and stay in the battle for his gracious kingdom when the world seems to be coming apart at the seams and new headlines pour in of another beheading, the outbreak of another deadly virus, one more school shooting, another article about girls and boys lured into human trafficking, more reports of injustice and violence on our streets, or abuse in homes and churches? Is God in this battle with us or not? Will hope survive when another church leader falls from grace before a watching world and the church itself seems small, weak, self-absorbed, and embroiled in internal fighting like an immune system gone awry? Can we trust God on those days when we don't even want to get out of bed because of the insurmountable personal challenges we're facing?

Like Barak, even the most seasoned believers need fresh fuel for faith and hope to thrive despite an onslaught of bad news. This battle sends a timeless message of hope in God who is in the battle with us and will ultimately prevail.

Barak's battle wasn't over with the rout of Sisera's army. As Israel's general, Barak cannot rest easy so long as Sisera is alive.

We must not pit Barak against Jael. It is a misreading of the text to suggest that Barak's pursuit of Sisera was motivated by his desire to win glory for himself or that Jael "has, in effect, conquered them both: Sisera by depriving him of his life, and Barak by depriving him of the honor that should have been his as the chosen deliverer."[41]

This misses the *aha* moment of the entire story. When Barak enters Jael's tent, sees Sisera lying dead at her feet, instead of feeling cheated of glory, Barak's faith in Yahweh is catapulted to a whole new level. No wonder he joins Deborah in celebrating the surprising and humanly impossible victory that Yahweh has won.

PATRIARCHY, BARAK, AND THE MALESTROM

Barak was a man of his times. He was born and raised within patriarchy, accustomed to the separate spheres of male and female, and aware of the advantages his maleness gave him over women. This man was no wimp but reached the rank of general in a vocation most cultures regard as the manliest of all—the military.

Contrary to all cultural expectations, Barak ends up sharing the limelight with two women who bracket his story by starting and finishing the war he fights in the middle. Perhaps the most "unforeseen situation" in this story is the fact that Barak seems completely unbothered by this cultural gender inversion. In fact, he welcomes, depends on, and celebrates the contributions of Deborah and Jael. What are we to make of this?

The vantage point that gives Barak deeper insight and makes gender a nonissue for him is that he sees the bigger picture. He does not minimize the ferocity of the battle he faces. Furthermore, this battle (as do all battles) comes at terrific cost for both winners and losers. We are mistaken to imagine Barak and his soldiers waltzing unscathed through their clash with nine hundred iron chariots. The battle was real. The fighting involved hand-to-hand combat. They saw the bloody damage from their swords. Even victory is horrific and costly.

The Bible isn't a collection of fairy tales where every story ends with a happily ever after. Biblical narratives are tragic, brutal, raw, and intended for the real world. Undoubtedly there were casualties. Barak must have seen friends die.

Anyone—in Barak's time or today—who grasps the scope and seriousness of the battle that was joined in Eden would never imagine telling any willing soldier—male or female— "We don't need you." That never seems to cross Barak's mind, and in fact both women in his story go beyond and above anything expected of a woman. All three of them give their all to this battle. Together they exemplify the Blessed Alliance where God brought victory over Israel's enemy through their mutually dependent efforts.

Barak's story reminds us that patriarchy is not God's design, but merely the cultural backdrop against which we see powerful glimpses of the gospel. Barak does not see the prophet Deborah or the death blow of Jael as threats to his manhood. He has seen too much. When God raises up, not just one, but two women to heroic status, Barak celebrates their actions. "Unforeseen situations" where women contribute and serve the purposes of God don't pose threats to men. They are instead serious threats to the Enemy. We get a hint of the original cultural mandate when the Bible shows us how God's sons and daughters can serve him together and then sing about it. But a man has to break free from the malestrom of patriarchy to see it.

Forty years of peace will follow. Then the depressing cycle of idolatry and rebellion, oppression, and the cry for deliverance in Israel will begin all over again. The Bible is for the real world — this very fallen world — where God's sons face fierce kingdom battles against the malestrom, the effects of the fall, and the temptation to displace God from the center. Barak's story points to a whole new kind of "unforeseen situation" where God's sons and daughters fearlessly join forces for his kingdom and end up praising God and singing each other's praises because God is creating something new and the kingdom of heaven is breaking in among us.

Another "unforeseen situation" occurs in the next chapter, where a man of great power collides with an *ezer*-warrior who, at first glance appears to be powerless. But to believe that is a big mistake.

DISCUSSION QUESTIONS

1. Describe an "unforeseen situation" you have witnessed or experienced. What was your reaction to it at the time? Why?

2. Do you relate to the negative views of Barak, Deborah, and Jael? Why or why not?

3. How does it change your understanding of this narrative to read it in terms of how God is revealing himself?

4. How do Barak, Deborah, and Jael exemplify a Blessed Alliance for God's purposes? How does their example offer wisdom to help us move toward stronger kingdom alliances among men and women within the body of Christ?

5. How did Barak battle the malestrom, and what does his story teach us about God's calling on his sons?

CHAPTER 5

THE POWER OF POWER

*"Nearly all men can stand adversity, but if you
want to test a man's character, give him power."*
—Abraham Lincoln

IT WAS WELL AFTER MIDNIGHT when the airport shuttle dropped
me off at my car in the hinterlands of an unlit Boston parking lot.
With a sense of relief, I got in my car, buckled up, and turned my
key in the ignition. Nothing happened. I turned the key again
and again and still nothing. I was tired, cold, and frustrated. As
I peered into the inky Boston blackness, my frustration turned
to fear. I was alone and in trouble, and I was afraid.

In a class at Wake Forest University women students
described the fears they live with and "what it feels like to have
to be constantly aware and on guard when they are alone, or
even in groups. It causes them to spend time planning strategies
to assure their safety."[1]

My middle-of-the-night predicament violated all those strategies. It was pitch dark. I was alone and completely vulnerable.
Instead of getting in my car, locking the doors, and traveling
safely home, I had to get out of my car and go find help. My
husband could not come to my rescue; he was over three hundred miles to the south slumbering peacefully in Pennsylvania
(although shortly to be awakened by his cell phone). I was still
an hour away from home. My closest friend was forty-five
minutes away. To make matters worse, I didn't have my Red

Sox baseball cap, which I'd been promised would guarantee my safety anywhere in Boston.

In the hours that followed, I was at the mercy of a parade of men who were total strangers, nearly twice my size, and significantly stronger. I don't usually resonate with Peter's description of women as the "weaker vessel,"[2] but I must confess, that night, I felt the comparison. As it turned out, every man I encountered that dreadful evening was a perfect gentleman. One man drove off in the darkness hauling my disabled car to some unknown auto repair shop; the others (there were several) went out of their way to ensure I made it home safely.

My story turned out okay. The men I encountered that night did not use their power advantage over me. Instead, they used their power to help, and so eventually I drove safely home in a rental car. But encounters between powerful males and powerless females in dark parking lots, in broad daylight, even behind closed doors in their own homes don't always turn out so well. It is well known that there is a demonstrable "connection between the masculine ideals of power and control, and widespread physical and sexual violence against women and girls."[3] Crimes against women are not crimes of passion, but of power.

We hear so many tragic stories of females who are on the receiving end of male power—abductions and rape, honor killings (sometimes for shaming their family by being raped), child marriages, sex trafficking, a disturbing variety of abuses—that the word "power" has come to be associated with domination, danger, violence, loss of agency, injustice, and evil.

So when we hear stories of men exercising power for good, we sit up and take notice. For instance, Bill Gates has converted his enormous wealth into financial power that is addressing poverty, education, health, and human rights issues around the world through the Bill and Melinda Gates Foundation. Or consider the recent *New York Times* report about the Afghanistan judge who refused to order the punishment of a hundred lashes for a ten-year-old girl raped by a mullah in his mosque. The judge refused to bow to cultural pressures or historic precedent and rendered his verdict emphatically, "She cannot commit adultery; she is a child. This is rape."[4]

THE GIFT OF POWER

Human power has always belonged in God's story, *not* as something humans should ever have to fear, but as a divine gift that is essential for us to fulfill our calling as image bearers. God's first command to his male and female image bearers was a glorious call to embrace and develop our God-given power. "Be fruitful and increase in number; fill the earth and subdue it. Rule over the fish of the sea and over the birds of the air and over every living creature that moves on the ground."[5] This is power as God intended.

In his insightful book *Playing God: Redeeming the Gift of Power*, Andy Crouch sets out a breathtaking view of power where God's image bearers are "agents of creativity in a universe designed to create more and more power."[6] Exercising power is a big part of what humans were created to do as we "bring the whole creation to its fulfillment."[7] Power is good as long as it is used to serve God's good purposes.

But nothing is worse than good power gone bad. Instead of fulfilling God's creation vision of flourishing, power turned dark and became a raging torrent in the malestrom. Disobedience brought a curse in which good power was twisted into bad power. The curse meant that the good power to rule and subdue the earth would be redirected to ruling and subduing the other, thus altering the dynamics between male and female and ultimately also between male and male. The gift of power became destructive—the stuff of horrifying global news reports: wars, shootings, homicide investigations, restraining orders, child abuse, and a myriad of other human rights violations, including polite and religiously sanctioned ways of defining relationships between males and females.

This bad power enthroned patriarchy, granting priority to fathers, husbands, and sons over mothers, wives, and daughters. The quest to "be a man" was redefined in terms of male prowess to conquer, control, and dominate others. Historically men have held physical, social, and political power over women—many in benign ways, but even "benign" falls woefully short of how God intends for us to use this gift. Young boys are socialized to adopt a "dominant, aggressive, controlling, and sexualized version of masculinity."[8] In extreme cases, this kind of masculinity weaponizes power and becomes the basis for social status and personal identity. Both ancient history and contemporary news reports are saturated with testosterone-driven power struggles in families, tribes, corporate offices, athletics, political chambers, and on battlefields. Instead of a gift that multiplies and blesses, power has been distorted into a zero-sum game where there's a scarcity of power, so "if someone has more, someone else has less ... [making God's image bearers] essentially competitors for power."[9]

From its inception, the church has never been safely roped off as a safe zone from the quest for power over others. Today, we have our own power struggles, and to our shame some of those struggles have spiraled into spiritual abuse and deeply divided competitive factions vying for control and protecting the powerful. If we are honest, too many of our evangelical churches are battlegrounds for power. Many of us have the wounds to prove it. This is not the way power is supposed to be used. There is a vivid alternative vision for good power. In order to see it, however, one may have to shed romantic dreams and enter into a culture very different from our own.

FAIRY TALE UNDONE

One of the strongest and possibly most surprising biblical examples of the good gift of power in action is in the Old Testament book of Ruth. Power isn't usually what comes to mind when most people think of this ancient narrative. According to traditional interpretations, it is a "beautiful love story"—a rags-to-riches romance that begins with a fortuitous meeting in Boaz's barley field where Ruth is gleaning and the pair end up falling in love. With the help of her mother-in-law Naomi's matchmaking maneuvers, Ruth's bold proposal, and Boaz's dexterity in overcoming legal obstacles, Boaz marries Ruth and rescues her from poverty, menial labor, and childlessness. It concludes tidily with the doting grandmother Naomi cradling Ruth's baby boy in her arms. The whole story ends up sounding like a Cinderella story, complete with a "happily-ever-after" banner billowing in the wind as the credits role at the end.

But this is anything but a Cinderella story. If we situate the story within the ancient patriarchal culture in which these events actually take place, a different story emerges. The context is a social system where sons are prized and daughters are a disappointment and an inconvenience to overcome. In societies like today's India, where the dowry is still practiced[10]—obligating a bride's parents to provide property or money to the bridegroom and his family—a daughter is a financial liability. Patriarchy is a worldview in which the value of a wife is gauged by the number of sons. This cultural context completely transforms how the three main characters in the book of Ruth are perceived, and a gripping story unfolds that puts male power and female powerlessness on a frightening collision course. First-time readers unacquainted with the story but aware of the cultural context would find the possibilities bone-chilling.[11]

The malestrom and the subject of power within this patriarchal context focus our attention on Boaz. No matter how one reads the book, the moment Boaz sets foot into the story, it is clear he is a powerhouse of a man who holds all the cards. He has wealth, power, and stature, and he is male. Born to a prominent family, he is culturally and politically empowered and expected to be a leader. One of the important questions lurking in the background is: Will Boaz use his power for the greater good or for selfish purposes?

In stark contrast to Boaz, Naomi and Ruth could not be in more desperate straits. Death struck three times in Moab (today's Jordan), where a grief-stricken Naomi buried her husband Elimelech and both of her sons (one who was married to Ruth). With the deaths of these three men, Naomi is stripped of everything that once gave her meaning and dignity as the successful mother of two sons. Naomi is aptly described as a female Job. Without sons, both Naomi and her widowed daughter-in-law, Ruth the Moabitess, are ranked as *zeros* on a patriarchal scorecard. But unlike Job, Naomi won't have the chance to begin again. The expiration of her childbearing years means her story is over. Her return to Bethlehem from Moab is not in hopes of building a new future, but to run out the clock.

Naomi in particular returns to Bethlehem overwhelmed by unmitigated despair: "The LORD's hand has gone out against me!"[12] Not only are Naomi and Ruth impoverished and marginalized, without husbands, sons, or any male relative to act in their defense, they are completely vulnerable. Anyone can exploit or abuse Naomi or Ruth with impunity. Even today, in patriarchal cultures, unprotected widows are one of the highest risk demographics—vulnerable to poverty, abuse, injustice, and sex trafficking.

So also in biblical times, even in Israel, unprotected widows were routinely exploited and abused. Brutality and injustice against the vulnerable incite the outrage of Yahweh and his prophets. Isaiah the prophet cries, "Woe to those who ... deprive the poor of their rights and withhold justice from the oppressed of my people, *making widows their prey* and robbing the fatherless."[13] Protections we assume—that I counted on the night I was alone in the airport parking lot—are completely missing in this story and missing in many places in today's world.

In reality, when Ruth ventured out to glean in the barley field, she was putting her life on the line. But for the starving poor, gleaning was the only option and a necessary risk to put food on the table. Naomi knew that, but undoubtedly suffered an anxiety-ridden day while she waited for Ruth's return. And it is pure fantasy to imagine Ruth wasn't fearful herself when she left the house and headed out into the fields.

MAN POWER

Boaz is introduced into the story as a man of "valor" (*hayil*). It is clear from the first mention that he is in every respect the polar opposite of Ruth and Naomi. The language employed to describe him speaks of wealth, strength, power, and might and conjures up images of an "elite warrior similar to the hero of the Homeric epic."[14] A towering figure by this description, like Barak, Boaz could easily be one of Israel's great military heroes as wars were common during the era of the judges. When Boaz arrives at his barley field and spots Ruth, the immigrant newcomer, the disparity between the two of them could hardly be greater. It is the meeting of male power and female powerlessness.

Boaz is a man of enormous power. He has power over property and people, and, as becomes evident later, he is also a powerful political leader of the community. But power comes with hard choices whether a man acknowledges this or not. On the one hand, he can wield these powers for himself and his growing estate in such a manner that his own power in Bethlehem increases. On the other hand, he can take a countercultural stance and use his powers to empower and look out for the powerless and vulnerable.

The power of wealth involves hard choices too. Both of the encounters between Boaz and Ruth take place on his turf—in his barley field where, after surviving the hard times of a prolonged famine, his workers are harvesting a good crop, and at his threshing floor, where Boaz is lying among the piles of winnowed barley guarding through the night what belongs to him. The challenge for Boaz will always concern how he will exert his powers and what he will do with the blessings Yahweh entrusts to him.

A Man Who Counters the Culture

A closer look at Boaz within his patriarchal context reveals the first battle Boaz must fight is to shed the misleading title of "romantic lead." That label poses insurmountable problems because romantic interpretations actually call into question Boaz's reputation as a man of high character.

For starters, scholarly consensus places Boaz in the same generation as Naomi. Both Boaz and Naomi address Ruth as "my daughter,"[15] an address that reveals they are Ruth's elders. If, as romantic interpretations allege, Boaz is an older bachelor, he has dishonored his family by neglecting his primary patriarchal duty as a son to marry and produce sons to secure the next generation. By this neglect, he dishonors his family and risks the legacy of the family name. Not only his family but the entire community would scorn a man like that. The modern notion of bachelors is foreign to patriarchy for it implies postponement of family responsibility. A man who didn't put his family's future first would be a disgrace to his family and never be regarded as a man of honor.

Another complication that is often overlooked is the inappropriateness of a wealthy landowner singling out and favoring with romantic intentions a young gleaner. Besides the fact that this represents a flagrant abuse of power, other deeply ingrained cultural issues are also involved. A man of high standing would never stoop to choose a wife among the scavengers in his field.

Patriarchy is a powerful cultural force that elevates family honor above personal desires. I am reminded of a man I met on a trip to India. He had sacrificed his right to marry the woman of his choice to accept an arranged marriage that proved disappointing to him. His decision was motivated by his concern to secure his younger sisters' hopes for advantageous marriages. No respectable man would want to marry the sister of a "wild" brother who disregarded cultural traditions. That's the way patriarchy works. It would be socially suicidal, not to mention laughable, for a man of Boaz's stature to choose a potential bride from among the scruffy gleaners in his field. That's called "marrying down." Ruth brings nothing to a marriage. As was painfully clear in the case of my Indian friend, patriarchal marriages are driven by opportunities to secure and enhance a family's prestige in society by cementing strategic social and political alliances with other wealthy, well-established families. Marriages are delicate and strategic arrangements that interconnect with the rest of the family.

But the death knell for the Cinderella version of this story is the fact that Ruth is certifiably barren. In a tight community like Bethlehem, it would be common knowledge that Ruth has been married to Naomi's son Mahlon for ten years and doesn't even have a daughter to show for it. The desperate quest for sons — a matter of family survival — overrides everything and will even prompt a man to add another wife or two or three. Patriarchy is polygamous. Ruth, however, lacks the one criterion any self-respecting patriarchal man requires in a wife. A man must have sons. Under patriarchy, Boaz would never merit the label *hayil* if he didn't already have sons or if his behavior bore the slightest taint of shirking family duty. In view of his cultural context, it is undoubtedly the case that Boaz is a married man or a widower with sons.

In the end, Boaz will redefine not only what it means to be a man, but he will raise the bar for what it means to be a man and a remarkable steward of power. Boaz gives us a glimpse of that missing chapter. But he won't get there without significant help. As it was for Judah and Barak, so also for Boaz, the help God sends comes from a woman. It's through his encounters with Ruth that he becomes a masculine exemplar of the kind of creative, flourishing, multiplying power of the gospel that the world so desperately needs.

LAW AND ORDER

I once described Boaz as "a buttoned-down man of impeccable conduct."[16] That description still holds and nowhere fits better than in his careful observance of the Mosaic law. Boaz is Israel's native born son. His parents raised him on the Mosaic law, and he knows his duty before the law. Evidence shows up immediately in the fact that gleaners are permitted in his field. Evidently he has regulars, which is probably why right away he notices a newcomer — Ruth the Moabitess, Naomi's daughter-in-law.

What draws his interest in Ruth is the fact that her reputation has preceded her. All Bethlehem was abuzz over Naomi's young immigrant daughter-in-law, who turned her back on any hope of security that her family of origin might have provided and forfeited everything to embrace Naomi's God and join her in a life of poverty and suffering. In Yahweh, Ruth had found the pearl "of great value,"[17] and she abandoned everything to follow him. Her actions had to make a strong impression on the people of Bethlehem who have grown accustomed to Yahweh. Her unpredictable, culturally unexpected choice on the road from Moab to Bethlehem won't be the last time this newly converted immigrant brings a fresh perspective to faith in Yahweh that Bethlehemites have known all their lives, as Boaz is soon to discover. The young woman who left Moab is not the same woman who arrives in Bethlehem.

Three specific Mosaic laws play a pivotal role in this story. The three laws governed social dynamics between the haves and have-nots. The Gleaning Law required landowners to open their fields to foreigners, widows, and orphans after the landowner finished harvesting his field.[18] During harvest, hired male harvesters cut the grain and left it lying on the ground. Female harvesters followed, gathering the grain into bundles to be carried to the threshing floor. The law allowed landowners one pass to clear their fields and stipulated that they leave the edges and corners of their fields uncut. Gleaners could come along behind and pick up whatever was left. The law didn't specify *how much* grain landowners were supposed to leave behind. This faced them with an inherent and healthy conflict of interest: How thoroughly should they clear the field? How wide is an edge? How big is a corner? How much to keep? How much to give away?

The other two laws address family relations in situations of loss. We encountered an early form of the Levirate Law[19] in the story of Judah and Tamar, which was later encoded in the Mosaic law. It applied to situations where a man died without a male heir and placed responsibility on the dead man's surviving blood brother to marry the widow and produce a son to take the dead man's place along with his inheritance in the family estate. This law reflects how alien the patriarchal culture of Israel is to us. In the opening scene of this story, Naomi makes a bitter reference to the Levirate Law,[20] which leaves her without hope. This explains why she emancipates her daughters-in-law from their obligation to accompany her back to Israel. "Why would you come with me? Am I going to have any more sons, who could become your husbands? Return home, my daughters; I am too old."[21]

The third law that informs the context of this story is the

Kinsman-Redeemer Law.[22] It is important to observe that this Jewish law is *not* about marriage, but centers on matters of *land and real estate*. It stipulated that if a man fell on hard times and was forced to sell his property, his nearest relative was to purchase his land to keep it in the family and maintain tribal boundaries.

Although the Levirate Law certainly provided safe haven for a widow who, like Naomi and Ruth, could end up out in the cold, the beneficiary of both of these family laws is *a man*: the deceased brother and the bankrupt male landowner. Furthermore, all three laws were a *call to sacrifice* financially for others. We are reminded once again that it is a disservice to portray Boaz as "getting the girl," when a deeper, gospel message is conveyed through his sacrificial actions.

But what is important to acknowledge—and what makes the powerful dynamics between Ruth and Boaz so incredibly fascinating—is the fact that neither of these family laws were legally applicable to Naomi or Boaz. Naomi, the widow in question, is postmenopausal. The land that belonged to her husband (Elimelech) lies dormant and will by default eventually become the property of the nearest kinsman-redeemer. Perhaps the most significant legal fact is that *none* of these laws is binding on Boaz, who is neither Elimelech's blood brother nor his nearest kinsman-redeemer. The fact of the matter is that this story is not about the irresistible pull of romance. It isn't even about legal obligations either. Something much deeper is going on in this story. It is a story about living on a completely different plane of existence where patriarchy and cultural traditions have no currency.

THE HUNGRY SIDE OF THE LAW

The malestrom suffers major setbacks in the barley field the first time Boaz encounters Ruth the Moabitess. This is where patriarchal concerns begin to wane. The prescribed patriarchal dynamics between male/female dynamics are inverted as Ruth takes the initiative with Boaz and he responds by backing her outrageous proposals with all his might, and a whole new brand of manhood begins to surface. By the time the story reaches the infamous threshing floor, this new order has taken hold.

Encounters between Boaz and Ruth contain the ingredients that in today's world all too often explode with violence and injustice. In this fallen world, combining male and female, rich and poor, powerful and powerless, valued and discarded, native born and immigrant, Jew and Arab,[23] is tantamount to mixing nitro and glycerin. To make matters worse, Ruth doesn't keep her head down and avoid a confrontation, which a woman of her low station in the culture would be well-advised to do. Yet instead of the deafening explosion one might expect, a Blessed Alliance forms between Ruth and Boaz that has kingdom repercussions to this day. The tide turns when Ruth takes the initiative and makes outrageous proposals with this powerful man.

Gleaning is a hand-to-mouth existence and competition could get rough among hungry gleaners. Ruth could easily take home next to nothing for a long day of gleaning. But Ruth doesn't want to take home scraps of grain to Naomi. She has vowed to take care of her mother-in-law and she will stop at nothing to see that she is fed. So she makes the audacious request of Boaz to break the gleaning rules. She asks permission to glean behind the male harvesters where there is plenty of grain on the ground.

Naomi is a pragmatist. She is concerned about what will become of her young immigrant daughter-in-law who most likely will outlive her. Ruth will end up alone, poor, and stranded in a foreign culture. She sends Ruth to the threshing floor to seek marriage. Naomi is seeking shelter for Ruth under the protection of a husband. It is important to note that after enduring ten agonizing years of Ruth's infertility, Naomi wouldn't be so cruel and selfish as to send Ruth to Boaz with the purpose of bearing a child. Far from being selfish, Naomi is making a costly sacrifice, for Ruth is all she has and she is willing to give her up to ensure her future. Naomi is seeking mercy from a man who has proven himself to be gracious to her daughter-in-law and so might be willing to take Ruth in. Bear in mind, we are dealing with a patriarchal culture where polygamy is accepted.

Ruth will follow her mother-in-law's instructions up to a point. But she will not be swayed from her vow. Without a son, Naomi's family is dying out—one of the greatest calamities for a family in the ancient patriarchal world. Ruth's proposal at the threshing floor calls Boaz to join her in fighting and sacrificing for the survival of the family.

In each encounter, Ruth is not thinking of herself, but putting herself at enormous risk in order to advocate for Naomi. She assumes responsibility for Naomi and is advocating for her. Ruth's trust in Yahweh's wing of protection emboldens and helps her gain the confidence she needs. She has the audacity to challenge Boaz's interpretation of all three Mosaic laws. Not only do her assertive actions violate cultural and social protocols (in both cases, Naomi probably would have stopped her), but her ideas imply the beliefs Boaz has held all his life are wide of the mark. It cannot have been easy for Boaz to hear Ruth's proposals. Accepting them would cost him a great deal.

It's difficult to imagine the heart-pounding courage this required, the huge risk Ruth is taking, or Boaz's radically unpatriarchal responses if we don't keep reminding ourselves this didn't happen in an American shopping mall or corporate city office. This story occurred in an ancient Near Eastern patriarchal culture much like today's Middle East. Every time she speaks, she risks abuse at the hands of male power. But Ruth is undeterred.

Conversations between the two of them boil down to the difference between the letter and the spirit of the law. Ruth lives on the hungry side of the law, and things read differently from that side of things. The letter of the law says, "Let them glean."

The spirit of the law says, "Feed them!" The letter of the law says, "Family responsibility falls on the shoulders of a blood brother and the nearest relative." But the spirit of the law says, "God calls his sons and daughters to sacrifice for one another."

Surprisingly, Boaz is neither dismissive nor defensive. No offense is taken. He doesn't pull rank on her either. In a breathtaking exhibit of the kind of manhood Jesus later embodies, Boaz takes her seriously and he listens. That alone is revolutionary. But Boaz doesn't stop there. He honors her initiatives. He listens and learns from the gleaner. Through Ruth, his eyes are opened to new possibilities for obedience to God, and he springs into action in ways that exceed her request. Conversations with Ruth free this staid and buttoned-down man of valor to throw his powers unreservedly behind her efforts.

In both encounters, he observes that Ruth isn't in this for herself. She's fighting for Naomi. She is looking to glean more than a few scraps of grain for her hungry mother-in-law. Boaz exercises his power on her behalf, and she returns home with twenty-nine pounds of winnowed barley — fifteen times what a male harvester could make in a single day. At the threshing floor, Ruth is not seeking a husband for herself (the protection Naomi meant for her to secure);[24] rather, she is actually fighting to rescue Elimelech and his family from extinction. In an innovative use of Mosaic law, Ruth combines the Levirate and Kinsman-Redeemer Laws in a proposal of marriage to a dumbfounded Boaz. She is asking for Boaz both to redeem Elimelech's land and to father a son for the sake of Elimelech's legacy. In an act of staggering faith, barren Ruth volunteers to bear a son. She offers herself as a surrogate mother on behalf of Elimelech's family and her postmenopausal mother-in-law.

Boaz doesn't disguise his astonishment. You can be certain he has never seen the likes of this young Moabite immigrant. He marvels at her lavish love for Naomi and describes her — not as a zero, but with words that attach the highest value on her. She is a woman *hayil*. He says it, and the whole community knows it. At this moment her worth flies off the charts.

But by incorporating the law in her proposal, Ruth makes this a legal matter. Elimelech has a nearer kinsman than Boaz who has rights and must be considered. But Boaz reassures her that, one way or another, he will make certain her request is granted.

At the city gate, the village governing center, Boaz assembles a quorum of elders and exerts his powers to settle the matter of Naomi's land and Ruth's proposal with Elimelech's nearest kinsman-redeemer, who spells out the risks of this high-stakes gamble. Rescuing Elimelech's property involves the outlay of large sums of money — siphoning off financial resources from his own estate to get Elimelech's land up and running again. If Ruth remains barren or only gives birth to a daughter, he stands to *double* his estate by acquiring Elimelech's land. But if she gives birth to a son, it is a losing investment and his own sons will inherit less.

Why neither the nearer kinsman nor any of the city elders dare question the irregular terms Boaz sets demonstrates just how powerful a man he is in the political arena. It is a risk the nearer relative can't afford to take. It will endanger his own estate.[25] Boaz exerts his political clout to ensure both Levirate and Kinsman-Redeemer laws are followed, even though the details are highly irregular. He does so with the most selfless intentions, putting his own estate at great risk for the sake of Elimelech, and the entire community knows it. It is a stunning gospel example of male power invested on behalf of those who have no power or voice in the community.

True to his word, he marries Ruth, and Yahweh "enabled her to conceive, and she gave birth to a son."[26] Boaz willingly accepts the cost and, as things turn out, pays a steep price for his decision.

FORCE MULTIPLICATION

In military usage "force multiplication" is a technical term that refers to an element that makes military action more effective than it would be without it. For example, in WWII, the British developed radar, which gave the advantage to Royal Air Force (RAF) in the Battle of Britain. It was precisely this victory that inspired Prime Minister Winston Churchill to say of the RAF, "Never in the field of human conflict was so much owed by so many to so few." A force multiplier (such as radar in the Battle of Britain) is the added factor that dramatically increases (hence "multiplies") military effectiveness.

When Boaz exerts his power for the good of Ruth and Naomi, both women flourish and kingdom power multiplies. The three of them together are more powerful than any one of them could possibly be alone. Good power is a force multiplier. Together, the three of them give a stunning example of the Blessed Alliance. And Boaz becomes an even more powerful figure at the ending than he was in the beginning, for "true power multiplies when it is shared."[27]

Boaz violates cultural norms of manhood when he responds to Ruth's initiatives and accepts her cultural and theological influence. He proves unwilling to allow patriarchal views of male power over women get in the way of listening, learning, growing, and changing. He is willing to be taught by her. A situation that easily could have gone badly for her (and in many cultures globally would have) puts in motion a history-altering series of events.

Boaz's power multiplies to empower Ruth to feed her mother-in-law and rescue Elimelech. Together the two of them empower a postmenopausal female Job to begin again—for Ruth gives her baby to Naomi, as the women rejoice, "Naomi has a son!"[28]

But even beyond these localized family issues, the powers of all three mushroom to accomplish more than any one of them ever realized. By facing their fears—of losing power, of taking risks, of losing God's love, of being shamed, abused, or getting hurt—and stepping out to make costly sacrifices. The three of them became kingdom agents who unknowlingly advanced God's purposes for the world. The genealogy at the end delivers the punch line: the family they all fought to save was the royal line of King David that would ultimately lead to Jesus.

Male power is one of the most lethal and dangerous forces at work in today's world. But male power also holds unimaginable potential for good—for empowering the powerless, shielding the weak, and promoting the flourishing God intends for his world. Whatever else it means to be the kind of man God created his sons to be, it means exerting power and making sacrifices for the good of others. Boaz's story also demonstrates the benefits of listening to someone who brings a different perspective. The next chapter takes us to consider men who battle the malestrom in the margins of society where men use power and privilege to prevail over other men.

DISCUSSION QUESTIONS

1. What makes a person powerful? What gave Boaz power versus Ruth and Naomi?

2. How does power create a conflict of interest for a man like Boaz?

3. How do Boaz's responses to Ruth's initiatives violate his culture's expectations and norms? How does he redefine what it means to be a person who possesses the gift of power?

4. How do Boaz's actions multiply power—his own and that of both Ruth and Naomi?

5. How did Boaz battle the malestrom, and what does his story teach us about God's calling on his sons?

CHAPTER 6

THE MARGINALIZED MAN

*"My hand is not the color of yours ... but the
blood that will flow from mine will be the same
color as yours. I am a man. God made us both."*
—Ponca Chief Standing Bear

CHAPEL WAS OVER, AND THE auditorium drained of college students heading for class like a tub of water when the stopper is pulled. I had just finished speaking at a leading Christian college on the power of the gospel in the story of Boaz and Ruth. That message never fails to strike a chord with women, and as expected, my time on campus included thoughtful follow-up conversations with college women.

What I didn't expect was that those who hung back to talk after chapel were three men—an Asian, African-American, and the son of Hispanic immigrants. Nor did I expect that all three of them felt a deep connection with Ruth, whose demographics as a poor Arab immigrant classified her as a minority and shoved her to the margins of the dominant Israelite society. Each student wanted me to know why her story hit a nerve with him. The point of connection they described wasn't from realities and experiences that occurred prior to college, but from marginalization they were experiencing within a Christian college environment. They spoke of social exclusion and how in a majority-white student body, the other young men in the college tended to choose their friends within their own ethnic group.

It wasn't the first time, after speaking about the marginalization of women, minority men told me from their own experiences, "I know exactly what you're talking about." Those conversations alerted me to a much wider continuum of injustice of men against men that at one end are often unintended and have nothing to do with violence. On the other end of the continuum there are unspeakable acts of violence and atrocities that men perpetrate against other men. We are painfully aware of the appalling numbers of men and boys who are trafficked as slaves for labor and sex and as soldiers. The problem is global and has deep roots that can be traced back to Genesis and to the descent of the malestrom.

One of the often ignored but most destructive consequences of the malestrom is the fact that not all men are beneficiaries of the powers of patriarchy but are, ironically, among the greatest casualties. Men not only create hierarchies over women, but "men create hierarchies and rankings among themselves according to criteria of 'masculinity.' "[1] Such criteria usually have nothing to do with a man's character or how he regards other people. It is fair to say that at one time or another, the majority of men end up on the losing end of this scheme. The fall and the curse that opened the door for men to rule over women ignited a dark ambition in the souls of men that extends a perverted sense of rule to their brothers.

It began with Cain's violent murder of Abel and escalated into the creation of tribes and empires, widespread oppression, and endless wars. Genocide, ethnic cleansing, massacre, holocaust, apartheid, discrimination, slavery, caste and class, racism, profiling, abuse, and elitism—these are just a short list of obscene concepts that inevitably take a terrible toll in the lives of men and boys. Expressions of male violence against other men have overrun the planet and dominate the news. They form a repeating cycle that plays out among schoolboys on playgrounds as well as among men on battlefields where violence is met with violence. If someone hits you, slug him back!

Patriarchy at its core is an unjust system that advantages and empowers some men and disadvantages and disempowers others. This is a double-edged sword since God's image is violated, not only by those who perpetuate violence, but also by the injustices they commit against the *imago dei* in others. From a global perspective, the majority of men get swept to the margins by birth, by the actions of someone else, or by their own self-destructive choices. The rest are always at risk. The very right of a man to call himself a man—even his very humanity—is under assault when another man asserts power and privilege over him.

For centuries, in North America and South Africa white men regularly addressed black men and slaves as "boy." The use of this word was the ultimate sign of disrespect and often more offensive than using the N-word. In the Jim Crow South, to call a black man a "boy" was intended as a verbal degradation of their manhood. That is precisely why the 1968 Memphis sanitation strikers, led by Rev. Dr. Martin Luther King Jr., wore signs saying, "I Am A Man!"

LONELY AT THE TOP

The tragic reality that confronts us is that there is a whole lot more room in the lower regions of patriarchy's male pyramids (and there are layers of them) than at the top. In fact, the top of a pyramid cannot exist without establishing and maintaining a well-populated base.

Ascendancy to the top often requires little more than the passive process of arriving through the birth canal into the advantaged demographic (or in strict patriarchal cultures, arriving ahead of your brothers). In essence, it amounts to winning the lottery at birth. Arriving with the preferred nationality, skin color, economic and social class, family pedigree, inner wiring, and access to education and opportunity means some are ahead of the game before they even know there is a game. From birth they have a place at the top that is theirs to lose. The same route also drops other males on the pyramid before they take their first small gasp of life. No one gets to choose where they will be born.

Exceptions happen. If a man lacking one or more of those prized qualifications possesses enough inner helium, star power, or skill in assimilating and/or navigating between two cultures, he may rise above the disadvantages of birth. In reality, however, few men are so lucky. Even then there can be limits, as a young Asian-American realized when he hit what researchers describe as the Bamboo Ceiling—"an invisible barrier that maintains a pyramidal racial structure throughout corporate America, with lots of Asians at junior levels, quite a few in middle management, and virtually none in the higher reaches of leadership."[2]

Within any given culture, male socialization is a factor in shaping one's self-perception. Many young men acquire their sense of masculinity from their locker room experiences. Male socialization all too often is bound up with becoming "a socially dominant alpha male who runs the American boardroom."[3] One son of immigrants described his life as "a study in alienation ... living on the border of two cultures, trying to bridge the gap created by different languages, different social expectations, and different values."[4] How is a man supposed to overcome years of upbringing or the inner wiring that put him out of step with society's standards of masculinity?

As a young boy, George Hosato Takei and his parents, along with many other loyal Japanese-American citizens, suffered a devastating marginalization when they were held in a Japanese Internment Camp during WWII. He attended school inside the camp where every day he saluted and pledged allegiance "to the flag ... with liberty and justice for all." The injustice of the experience left deep wounds later compounded by the media's tendency to stereotype Asian men as comedic idiots or martial arts experts. Takei's parents told him that his role as *Star Trek's* Lieutenant Hikaru Sulu, helmsman of the USEnterprise, was the first time they were proud of how an Asian man was portrayed.

When America's founding fathers declared their independence from British rule, the liberties and protections they formalized into law didn't extend to the African slaves they owned or to Native Americans whose land they now possessed. History that seems long past lives on in "the legacy of slavery in today's criminal justice system."[5] A 2012 report demonstrates that there are two systems of criminal justice in the US. "Racial minorities are more likely than white Americans to be arrested; once arrested, they are more likely to be convicted; and once convicted, they are more likely to face stiff sentences."[6] Glaring inequities surface when white youths whose middle class parents can afford a good lawyer are hustled off to a wilderness camp, while a minority youth charged with the same crime is assigned an overworked court appointed public defender and gets slapped with a felony and a prison sentence.

Margins in the Pews

We rightly bemoan the many injustices in American society and shake our heads with disapproval. But the church community has its own dual groupings of those who are in power and those who are relegated to the margins.

Protestant Reformers were adamant about the need to stop elevating clergy over laity. But that distinction remains alive and well within the church and is often the basis for ranking men. A friend of mine spoke from personal experience when he observed that men are marginalized every Sunday in our American evangelical churches. I thought immediately of the handyman I knew whose highly sensitive pastoral antennae could detect the hurting person no one else saw and reach out—sometimes in incredibly down-to-earth practical ways. If someone went missing, he'd track them down. It was a gift to be in that man's orbit. But he was never tapped for leadership of the flock and wouldn't have thought of himself that way, even though that was exactly his gifting and what he was in fact doing.

Some may think ordination is "a women's issue." But actually, it's a pretty serious "men's issue" too. Within the church, usually the men who rise to prominence are ordained pastors with seminary degrees or who hold some other official leadership position in the church or in Christian ministries and organizations. I'm thankful for these men. In fact, I'm married to one. But God has blessed his church with a lot of other men whose gifts we need. Yet, if a man doesn't enter the sanctuary with the right resume, the right financial portfolio, an intact family, or the ability to wax eloquent in front of an audience, he can easily become invisible and never have anyone wonder (or even wonder himself) what spiritual gift he is bringing.

A corporate executive noted there's little acknowledgment of men who head out Monday morning into the workplace and little if any vision that they are serving God *by the very work* they do. Women feel this too. "Secular" work doesn't rise to the level of "official ministry" or church volunteerism.

APOSTLE OF THE MARGINS

Matthew the apostle was born in the margins. As a Jew under first-century Roman occupation he was a member of the oppressed Israelite population. "To put it simply, most Jews of Jesus's day did not believe that the exile was really, properly over ... pagan foreigners were still ruling over them. They were still slaves even in their own land."[7]

Matthew was also marginalized as an apostle. Despite the fact that his gospel comes first in the New Testament, he is one of the Bible's missing men—one of several forgotten apostles eclipsed by the more prominent apostles, Peter, James, and John, and even by the late arrival, Paul. Sometimes Matthew even goes missing from the gospel that bears his name. Yet, as I started thinking more about Matthew's story, I began to notice how his story and social alienation smolder beneath the surface of his writing. Matthew doesn't write from the privileged position of a cultural elite, but from the point of view of an outcast rejected by society, who was unexpectedly embraced by Jesus. I doubt he ever got over that.

There were also other darker reasons Matthew was sentenced to the periphery of Jewish society. His choice of vocation may have been a shortcut to financial success. Unfortunately, wealth does not always add up to community prominence and an entrée into the upper echelons of society. In Matthew's case, his career choice was his ticket to the bottom and to social ostracism. That's where he was when Jesus found him.

Caught up in one of the most notorious, unethical, yet lucrative professions in Israel, Matthew was a charter member of the club of men of whom it is fair to say, "Greed got the best of them." His job entailed collecting taxes that Rome levied on Jewish citizens. That alone was enough to make Jewish people hate him. But as the deal went down, tax collectors would pocket whatever extra they could squeeze out of hapless taxpayers or by extorting payoffs by falsely accusing merchants of smuggling. Of course this was devastating to the poor, but as long as the Romans got their taxes, they turned a blind eye to this egregious practice. One could get rich this way—filthy rich.

Like today's golden-parachute CEOs, Matthew's financial prosperity came at a steep personal price. First-century Israelite tax collectors were among the most despised members of Jewish society. He may have had an impressive portfolio, but respectable God-fearing Jews shunned him.

In the eyes of Jewish citizens who chafed under the boot of Rome, tax collectors were traitors of the lowest sort for exploiting their fellow Jews and for collaborating with the Roman oppressors—who no doubt looked down on them too. Interacting with Gentiles and handling pagan money classed them as religiously unclean. Pharisees spoke of them with utter disgust. The New Living Translation uses "scum" to express how Pharisees viewed them.[8] No doubt Jesus' other disciples found it hard to stomach the admission of a tax collector into their inner circle.

No one loves to pay taxes. It's one of the most contentious topics on the American political scene, and I daresay is a big issue around the globe. My grandfather was a successful rice miller who found out during the Depression what it was like to put cardboard in his shoes because the soles had worn so thin. But things did turn around, and he weathered the economic storm. As things got better he used to say, "Pay your taxes and be thankful."

Paying a fixed percentage in taxes is one thing, and even that can be maddening. It's a whole different story to be dealing with a tax collector you know is getting rich by cooking the books so that you pay more. In Matthew's day, it was common knowledge that tax collectors were pulling these kinds of shenanigans. Matthew was gouging his fellow Jews to increase his own bank account and, to make matters worse, he could only do this by collaborating with the occupying Roman forces.

Roman government officials sold tax collection franchises to the highest *Jewish* bidder. These "chief" tax collectors (Zacchaeus was one)[9] hired other tax collectors who would owe them a cut of their "earnings." Their vocation has been likened to a cross between "a pyramid scheme and a protection racket."[10] Matthew was a nasty blend of Bernie Madoff, who pulled off one of the largest financial frauds in US history, and Whitey Bulger, Boston's ruthless crime boss/FBI informant. Tax collectors got rich by taking money for themselves that rightly belonged to the people and playing both ends against the middle—that is, by doing the dirty work for Roman officials while at the same time becoming part of the systemic corruption and exploitation oppressing Israel. Unlike Madoff and Bulger, Matthew didn't end up behind bars. Instead, he and his cronies were getting away with their crimes and enjoying the profits. Everybody knew it.

When Matthew shows up in the gospels, he's working a Capernaum tollbooth under the auspices of Herod Antipas, who had jurisdiction over Galilee and was also the merciless despot who beheaded John the Baptist.[11] The tollbooth was stationed either at the exit to Capernaum or more likely along the nearby major trade route, the *Via Maris*, where merchants would be traveling. Proximity to the Sea of Galilee meant he was levying taxes on trade merchandise "as well as on fish caught by the commercial fishermen in the lake."[12] Undoubtedly, Peter, James, and John had already had unpleasant dealings with Matthew.

It must have evoked some wary glances when Jesus called "Matthew the tax collector" to be his disciple along with the other disciples—men Matthew had cheated, men who now had less because Matthew had more. The rugged fishermen Peter, James, and John no doubt found this unexpected development hard to swallow. Throw in Simon the Zealot, and Matthew had better sleep with one eye open when traveling with the Twelve. What was Jesus thinking?

GOSPEL DEMOLITION

Matthew's road to wealth trapped him even deeper in the margins and limited his social options to those of his own ilk. His everyday experiences mirrored Jesus' parable of the Good Samaritan. Matthew was like the man that the priest and Levite avoided by walking on the other side of the road. He was an outcast—truly by his own doing. For Jesus to welcome the miscreant Matthew from the margins was a revolutionary act of the first magnitude. It violated all Jewish social norms and even put his most devout followers on edge. The disciples may have perceived themselves as radicals, but the inclusion of Matthew demonstrates they were not nearly as radical as Jesus. His gospel cannot be domesticated.

One of the first things Jesus' gospel does is shatter the masculine pyramid. In fact, you could say he turns that pyramid upside down by giving *priority* to people in the margins. We can trace this pattern back to the Exodus, where Yahweh's heart was set on the suffering Hebrew slaves whose cries of injustice reached his ears and whom he was bent on freeing. Reading Matthew's gospel and knowing what kind of man he had been make it impossible to sustain the illusion that the advantages of birth, wealth, privilege, and power give any one man value above another in God's eyes. Jesus doesn't gravitate toward the rich, the elite, the socially prominent, or the powerful. His disciples are ordinary, uneducated working-class men. To this day we know next to nothing about most of them. They weren't "the men to watch" in first-century Israelite society where all eyes were on the religious leaders and the Roman powers that be.

The turning point for Matthew comes when Rabbi Jesus shows up in the margins—at the tollbooth—where the despised, unclean, miserly tax collector is busy raking in profits for himself and no doubt trying to ignore demeaning looks and disparaging comments from the people he is exploiting. Then, much to his utter astonishment, Matthew hears a voice of welcome, an invitation to enter into a very different stratum of society.

"FOLLOW ME."

It is difficult to fathom what those two words from Jesus meant to Matthew, so accustomed to being treated like the worst of the worst. Matthew got up, "left everything,"[13] and followed Jesus.

Matthew is one of several biblical characters (like Rahab the harlot and Simon the leper) who never seemed to shake their past. Although other gospel writers graciously drop the derogatory descriptor, Matthew stubbornly identifies himself as "Matthew the tax collector."[14] He seems to want readers to know his backstory. In contrast, Mark and Luke identify the tax collector as "Levi"[15] and the apostle simply as "Matthew."[16] Some modern scholars think Mark and Luke chose to use "Levi" instead of "Matthew" simply because Matthew (like Simon Peter and Saul/Paul) had more than one name. Perhaps they did it to erase Matthew's past and affirm him as a changed man.

Jesus' invitation to Matthew wasn't an impetuous decision. It was a strategic move that was consistent with Jesus' mission. In the choice of a man everyone loathed, Jesus' kingdom is breaking through, upending fallen ways of thinking, of ordering society, and of ranking men. Matthew is transformed into a new kind of man who seeks a new kind of kingdom—a kingdom with a "not of this world" ethos. This alien kingdom has no walls or class system. It doesn't rank or divide human beings by gender, ethnicity, or any demographics. King Jesus is a radical—he knocks down all barriers between male and female, male and male, Jew and Gentile, as well as slave and free. Amid these radical revisions, Jesus also redefines what it means to be a man. The inclusion of a man like Matthew into the inner circle of Jesus' disciples is a striking demonstration that patriarchy does not belong to the kingdom of King Jesus.

"Follow me!" is, in fact, a call to radical change. The call to follow is necessarily connected to Jesus' summons, "Repent, for the kingdom of heaven has come near."[17] The Greek word for "repent" means "to change your mind" or "make a U-turn." It's not enough to quit the corrupt tax collection business and find a more suitable line of work, although that was surely a start for Matthew. Nor is repentance confined to occasional moments of remorse over past lapses along the way, although that is important too. These narrow definitions of repentance can leave us thinking repentance is for others or restricted to isolated events, instead of a lifestyle of ongoing change and redirection. This is where the Pharisees were off track. By careful living they would have no need for repentance. Matthew, however, had no problem realizing he needed to repent.

The call to follow Jesus is not magical. It marks the beginning of a long journey that entails working hard at change, at shedding the kingdom-of-this-world entanglements layer by layer, and making intentional strides toward becoming a new and radically different kind of man. Matthew's calling is a revolutionary act of defiance against the cultural norms of society. When Jesus said his kingdom is not of this world, he meant it, and the inclusion of Matthew demonstrates it.

THE VIEW FROM THE MARGINS

Jesus' call to Matthew undoubtedly brought about a thawing in the frozen heart of the tax collector. As an outsider's outsider to be welcomed into this traveling band of Jesus followers would have awakened in him a proclivity to latch on to certain statements that were especially nourishing to him. The personal experiences of the other gospel writers certainly informed the particular events and sayings they reported. Matthew was no different.

From his own personal experience, he picked up on the priority Jesus placed on the poor, the hungry, and disenfranchised. Matthew's gospel displays a noticeable tendency to include stories where Jesus engages those who live in the shadows of Jewish society. At the very outset of his gospel account in the genealogy of Jesus, Matthew uniquely names four Gentile women whose race and gender (not to mention Rahab's past history as a Canaanite prostitute) classed them as outsiders in Jesus' day. Matthew was the only gospel writer to include them.

Of the four gospels, Matthew alone includes the parable of the two sons where Jesus declares to the chief priests and elders: "Truly I tell you, the tax collectors and the prostitutes are entering the kingdom of God ahead of you."[18] It is not difficult to understand why this parable struck a chord with Matthew.

Only Matthew recounts Jesus' parable comparing the kingdom of heaven to the pearl of great price that a merchant discovered and "sold everything he had and bought it."[19] That was Matthew's story too. The parable echoes the Sermon on the Mount, where Jesus declared: "For where your treasure is, there your heart will be also."[20]

As a notorious traitor to his own people, Matthew must have carried deep regrets his entire life. One can easily imagine how he must have cherished the sweet words of Jesus for himself and longed for others to hear: "Come to me, all you who are weary and burdened, and I will give you rest."[21] As a social outcast, Matthew would have seized upon the powerful words of Jesus: "knock and the door will be opened to you."[22] Only those who know what it is like to be an outsider understand the need to knock. Because he was a man of the margins, Matthew alone was led to recount such generous words of inclusion.

Nor is it surprising that Matthew writes a lot about money and treasure. He absorbed Jesus' teaching on high finance that exposed the human preoccupation with acquiring and consuming as dangerous barriers to the kingdom of God. It ought to give pause to those of us who are blessed with so much when Jesus states unequivocally that "it is easier for a camel to go through the eye of a needle than for the rich to enter the kingdom of God."[23] Instead of being deeply troubled about the predicament Jesus says we're in, we try to soften his words to mean less than he intended, when Jesus "depicts the largest animal in Palestine (a camel) going through the smallest hole (the eye of a needle)"[24] to make his point.

It's reassuring to know that Jesus pulled Matthew, Joseph

of Arimathea, and Nicodemus through that tiny hole. But it is entirely possible (and Jesus seems to suggest this) that if Matthew's great wealth had brought him the hoped-for status and celebrity instead of misery and disdain, he, like the rich young ruler, might have been curious about Jesus, but would have found it hard to forsake what he had acquired to follow a homeless rabbi like Jesus.

GUESS WHO'S COMING TO DINNER?

Jesus drew Matthew out of the margins. But like so many escapees who breathe the fresh air of their dignity and worth as God's image bearers, Matthew's first recorded act as a Jesus follower was not to distance himself from his old friends, but to go right back into the margins to lead them out. He hosts a great feast for Jesus[25] and invites the only crowd he knows will come—"many tax collectors and sinners."

There is some uncertainty regarding who the "sinners" were. Some think they were prostitutes. If that is true, the dinner assembles a chilling combination of wealthy exploiters (tax collectors) and the utterly desperate (prostitutes) who were also thought to be servicing the Romans. Others suggest the "sinners" might have been Gentiles (a tax collector collects friends wherever he can find them). In a sense, it doesn't really matter. Jesus and his disciples are breaking bread with the marginalized and the unclean. They are flagrantly crossing social, religious, and cultural boundaries. Who knows how many tax collectors and "sinners" ultimately followed Jesus because they met him at the dinner in Matthew's house?

For Jesus and his disciples to be socializing with this crowd created a shock wave that rippled out from dinner guests (including his own disciples) to onlookers like the Pharisees. In the ancient world, sharing a meal carried much greater significance than it does in our world, for it implied acceptance, identity, and fellowship. This is one reason Jesus called his followers to remember him by sharing a meal together. Jesus was well aware of how his actions would be perceived, but remained unfazed. Evidently Jesus enjoyed evenings like this, for his critics mocked him as a "glutton and a drunkard, a friend of tax collectors and sinners."[26] But his actions that evening drew fire from the Pharisees who disapproved of his association with Matthew and his unseemly caste and were quick to point out the utter incongruity of a Jewish rabbi and his disciples eating with unclean rabble like this.

Pharisees are often portrayed as narrow-minded, kill-joy bigots. But in fact, they were highly respected Jewish leaders with very decided views of what it meant to be Jewish and a fierce determination to safeguard the purity and prerogatives of Israel. Sharing a meal with unclean people violated the Pharisaic notions of "Jewish set-apartness"[27] that distinguished the chosen people from the rest of the world. According to the Pharisees, God's people are a bounded set that excludes traitors, extortionists, and unclean people like Matthew.

Alarmed by Jesus' conduct, the Pharisees interrogate his disciples. "Why does your teacher eat with tax collectors and sinners?" Their objections were based on a dichotomy that Jesus refuses to accept. This issue becomes a major theme in Matthew's gospel, namely, that Jesus didn't come simply to save souls and tidy up the place. He came as King to overthrow the world's fallen, competitive, "us versus them" way of doing things. He is ushering in a whole new way of being human and of being male. He is intent on recovering God's image bearers and leading us back into the missing chapter and to a world without margins. The Pharisees have lost sight of the fact that Yahweh's covenant with Abraham included his son Ishmael and Abraham's slaves and was a global vision for blessing the nations.

Jesus' reply points to why his welcoming words are often heard first in the margins. "It is not the healthy who need a doctor, but the sick." Those who suffer injustice and exclusion, who are confined to the fringes and live on the receiving end of those who exert power over them, are the ones who know the world is profoundly broken and are looking for God to intervene. Plantations owners aren't the composers of the deep laments and longings for God that are embedded in the spirituals that came from the slaves. These masters were humming tunes that celebrated the "land of cotton."

HESED-MEN

Jesus isn't finished. Like a good rabbi, Jesus gives his critics a homework assignment to "go and learn what this means: 'I desire mercy, not sacrifice.' For I have not come to call the righteous, but sinners."[28]

"Mercy" is the rich Hebrew word *hesed*—one of the most potent words in the entire Bible and the bedrock of God's people. At its core, it describes God's heart for them. No English word captures the meaning of *hesed*, so Hebrew translators chose from words like "kindness," "mercy," "loyalty," "loving-kindness," "loyal, steadfast, unfailing (or just plain) love." These words certainly touch on the meaning, but even collectively don't do *hesed* justice. *Hesed* is a "love-your-neighbor-as-yourself" brand of living—an active undeserved love for others that is both costly, yet unrelenting.[29] Or, as one children's author put it, "Never Stopping, Never Giving Up, Unbreaking, Always and Forever Love."[30]

Jesus and his kingdom are characterized by *hesed*. The pharisaic concept of manhood is bound up in avoiding any taint that might rub off on them by associating with the wrong people. They have missed the heart of God's commands—that the love of God cannot be separated from love of neighbor. Men who follow Jesus will be *hesed*-men.

A New Genesis

Matthew opens his gospel with a zinger. It is true that most readers don't think of a genealogy as a compelling entrée to the story of Jesus. But they would be mistaken. Matthew's opening line includes startling language that for English readers gets lost in translation. Any first-century Greek-speaking Jewish audience familiar with the Old Testament would pick up on what he's saying right away.

The second word of Matthew's gospel is the Greek word *genesis*. English translations give us "ancestry," "family history," "genealogy," "birth," or "generations." Although these are all valid translations, they fail to make the connection Matthew is making between his gospel and the first book of the Bible: Genesis. Douglas Hare explains that Matthew's phrase,

> "the book of the *genesis* of Jesus Christ," is strongly reminiscent of the Greek version [the Septuagint] of Gen. 5:1, "the book of the *genesis* of human beings," and Gen. 2:4, "the book of the *genesis* of heaven and earth." By imitating these two phrases, Matthew intended perhaps to remind his readers that in Jesus Christ, God had made a new beginning. (emphasis original)[31]

Other commentators agree that "for the first readers of Matthew, [this language] called attention also to the birth (*genesis*) not only of Jesus, but of *the whole new order to which that birth gave rise*" (emphasis added).[32] With a little help from Hollywood, Professor Hare calls Matthew's gospel, "Genesis II, the Sequel."[33]

Matthew is doing a whole lot more than identifying ancestors or drawing a family tree. He is connecting the dots from Genesis to Abraham to David to Jesus and establishing that what comes next climaxes God's mission to redeem his world and put us all back on mission. Matthew's gospel launches with a powerful word of hope, namely, that God has not given up. His original creation vision is still alive and well, and Jesus is the long-awaited King and the hinge on which all of human history turns.

The genealogy not only establishes Jesus as the rightful heir to King David's throne, it connects Jesus and his gospel to the entire sweep of Israel's history. Israel's call to restore God's kingdom on earth is now squarely on the shoulders of Abraham's descendant, Jesus, who will fulfill the Abrahamic and Davidic covenants and succeed where Israel has failed. Matthew's emphasis on the "kingdom of heaven" and on Jesus' fulfillment of Old Testament prophecy underscores the central role of Jesus in bringing the entire Old Testament to fulfillment. But the kingdom Jesus brings is unrecognizable to the fallen world of the malestrom. Jesus is recovering a whole new, long-forgotten way of being human, of living as God's image bearers, of being male.

In the eyes of the Pharisees, Jesus was failing to live as a true Jew, which Jesus was—a true Israelite. The Pharisees lost sight of what God's kingdom is all about—especially how it revolutionizes how people care for one another. They were settling for a system of laws and national identity. Jesus is a contradiction to all of that, and Matthew who looks on from the margins is in a perfect position to see it. His gospel serves up a contrast between the kingdom the Pharisees desired and the true kingdom of King Jesus. He contrasts the righteousness of the Pharisees—a righteousness they had mastered, but that heaped scorn and hopelessness on him—with the righteousness of Jesus. Nowhere is Jesus' kingdom expressed more starkly or in more unsettling and humanly unattainable ways than in the Sermon on the Mount, for which Matthew held a front-row seat.

MEEKNESS AND MANHOOD

Read honestly, the Sermon on the Mount uncovers the chasm that followers of Jesus are called to traverse — the glaring gap between God's ways and our ways. It gives us a startling glimpse at the missing chapter (the chapter that contains the way God's image bearers are to live). It offers a radically different kingdom view of what it means to be a man in God's world. It's an upside down way of looking at how the world does things and a huge stretch to imagine living into that ethos without the help of Jesus and his Spirit.

Moving beyond the letter of the law to the spirit in shocking and revolutionary ways, Jesus undoes the world's value system that exalts one man over another. He completely dismantles all of the criteria that make men culturally important. "Blessed are the poor" undermines the notion that a man's earning power and bank account give him significance. It also points us to those who help us see the forces of injustice and evil that are rampant in God's world. Those who have suffered in the margins see the world differently. Meekness, mercy, purity of heart, peacemaking, and "hunger and thirst" — a craving for righteousness/justice (both in what they do and what they experience) — these describe the kind of masculinity God blesses. Jesus is clear that these character traits won't win the world's admiration or help a man summit a masculine pyramid that should never exist in the first place. But they win the Creator's blessings — the highest accolades of all.

What went through Matthew's mind as he heard Jesus teach these things? How completely are his heart and his whole value system being rebooted? And how is Jesus emancipating him from the downward drag of the malestrom that convinced him he was "scum" and trapped him in the bottom of the pyramid Jesus flattens here? In the words of N. T. Wright, "When God wants to change the world, he doesn't send in the tanks. He sends in the meek, the mourners, those who are hungry and thirsty for God's justice, the peacemakers."[34]

Jesus' message has a double-barreled impact on Matthew who lived at both ends of the fallen world system. He had unjustly oppressed others, even the poor, and was himself a target of abuse, discrimination, and exclusion. Matthew presents a Jesus who does not inaugurate a kingdom of weakness, but a new kind of power that doesn't flinch in the face of evil but also refuses to engage on evil's terms. Men like Matthew, who are listening to Rabbi Jesus, are hearing Jesus redeem and redefine masculinity according to the kingdom of heaven. This is a brand of masculinity that breaks the cycle of violence with mercy/*hesed* and peacemaking. This redefines power in far more subversive terms.

During a trip to Africa, I met another three men: two Africans and a Pakistani. All three were subjected to unspeakable injustices and brutal violence at the hands of other men. One lost his father, who was tortured and murdered by Islamic terrorists. A second lost many members of his family and his church who were slaughtered during the Rwandan genocide. The third was beaten and seriously injured by a mob of Islamic students who blamed him for something he didn't do. All three men were on the receiving end of violence and injustice. All three endured fierce battles of soul that were intensified by ongoing encounters with people connected to the injustices they suffered. All three battled the natural anger and hatred that would rise up in anyone's heart as a result.

But these men follow Jesus, and so all three chose a much harder path. All three broke the cycle of violence and injustice the malestrom perpetuates. They forgave their enemies and lived out that forgiveness in tangible ways—forging strong friendships with Muslims, living side-by-side in friendship with Hutu neighbors who had blood on their hands, and taking action to ensure those Muslim students could complete their education. The world doesn't have categories for this kind of manhood. The brand of kingdom power those men possessed and the freedom they gained was unearthly. Their stories are reason for renewed hope in this dark world and evidence that God is alive and at work in the lives of individual men.

Matthew's gospel takes us deeper into the world of men and what he was learning from Jesus. In the next chapter, Matthew unpacks the contrast between the righteousness of the Pharisees and the righteousness of Jesus in the story of a man who battles the malestrom's confining definitions of manly roles that hinder God's call on a man's life.

DISCUSSION QUESTIONS

1. What male power pyramids do you observe within your own cul-
    ture—in the public sphere, the social sphere, the workplace, and the
    church? What determines who's on top and who's below?

2. How did Jesus violate and confront the power status quo embraced by
    Matthew, Jesus' other disciples, and the Pharisees when he called Mat-
    thew to follow him?

3. How does the new *Genesis* that Matthew's gospel introduces radically
    transform human relationships, beginning with the inclusion, recov-
    ery, and redeployment of Matthew himself? What are the implications
    for today?

4. How did Jesus underscore the human/relational dimension of his
    kingdom when he sent the Pharisees away to figure out the meaning of
    "I desire mercy/*hesed*, not sacrifice"?

5. How did Matthew battle the malestrom, and what does his story teach
    us about God's calling on his sons?

CHAPTER 7

GENDER ROLE REVERSAL

*"The next time you see a father out
shopping with his kids, you might need
to check your assumptions."*
—Jennifer Ludden, NPR

SOME ACCOLADES ARE BOTH A blessing and a curse. Australian actor Chris Hemsworth, famed for his role as Thor, the muscular hammer-wielding superhero, landed on the cover of *People Magazine* as the 2014 "Sexiest Man Alive." I always find myself wondering who makes this decision and according to whose taste? In any case this designation has become something of a cultural benchmark of male attractiveness and is no doubt a career booster for Mr. Thor. The accolade comes at a cost, however, as the media becomes a free zone of rampant sexist comments about the winner—the very kind of talk that women have been fighting against for themselves for decades and that now reduce masculinity to the "ornamental." What kind of awful double standard are women being asked to perpetuate against men by invitations to "Sneak a peek at what Hollywood's hottest guys have been hiding under their shirts"?

Women aren't the only ones who are objectified.

Nor are women alone in being confronted with unrealistic standards of measurement. The annual "Sexiest Man Alive" contest celebrates a state of hyper-muscularity and soaring celebrity few men have the time, resources, or desire to attain, and that in time will be overtaken in all awardees by crow's-feet, saggy knees, and too many aches to count. Sexy has a short shelf life. The ornamental standards may work for some, but a lot of men have grown weary of hiding the fact that they don't or won't or can't conform to the reigning definition of masculinity, whatever that evolving definition may be.

This weariness is also creating a brand new demographic as stay-at-home dads (formerly known as Mr. Moms) are on the rise. These dads are no longer hiding the fact that their wives are the breadwinners and they are "manning" the home front, the kitchen, and the kids. They're proud of what they're doing and want the world to know. Big changes are happening for women. But men are changing too.

At least five different couples in my circle of friends are operating under this arrangement, as the stay-at-home dad becomes a demographic in the church. In fact, although the "stay-at-home dad" wasn't common parlance when our daughter was born, during the first year of her life, my husband was a trailblazer for the stay-at-home dad movement. I was the breadwinner while he stayed home to study for doctoral exams and rock, feed, and play with the baby. Rather than viewing that year as an embarrassing chapter of his life that diminished his manhood, Frank's unabashed assessment of his experience was, "Men are missing out."

Not only do a lot of fathers agree with Frank, so do a lot of kids. When a pediatrician asked a nine-year-old boy how he felt about his dad being home fulltime, the reply was unequivocal: "The happiest day of my life was when my dad came home from work and told me that he was going to stay home and take care of us from then on."[1] Having just started kindergarten, a five-year-old came home and announced, "Mommy, did you know in some families that the daddy goes to work?"[2]

Today, fathers have become more actively involved in parenting their children than any previous generation. A 2014

Pew Research report indicates that overall, the time dads are now spending with their children has tripled from a generation ago[3] — which is good news for the entire family. The days of Walt and June Cleaver are long gone, and growing numbers of dads "have raised their hand to become the chief household officer."[4] According to the Pew study, the number of fathers at home with children in the United States doubled between 1989 and 2010. "This role reversal — women as primary breadwinners, men as primary caregivers — has been gradual but significant in this country."[5] In about 40 percent of households, women now bring home the bacon and roughly two million men are stay-at-home dads.[6] These numbers don't reflect fathers who work part time or single dads who are juggling work and family.

Fathers are rocking their babies to sleep, cheering wildly at soccer games, wiping tears and little noses, making peanut butter sandwiches for their kids, singing "Let It Go" with their daughters, and learning to tie ribbons in their little girls' hair. A medical doctor told me that her role reversal only made sense because she was able to produce more income and besides, her husband was more nurturing with their children. Such marriages are not the norm, and it still is the case that the culture associates masculinity with a man's occupation and role as the family breadwinner. Tension can mount in double income families when a wife earns more than half of the family income. Although men may "applaud their spouses when they help to bring home the bacon, husbands aren't always as enthusiastic when women start bringing home the filet mignon."[7]

Today, not only have these stay-at-home dads come out in the open, they're getting organized. They're even forming support groups, like the *National At-Home Dads* reported by the *New York Times* in "The Brotherhood of Stay-at-Home Dads."[8] Dads are banding together to overcome their social isolation, share ideas, discuss parenting and educational issues, and give each other the kind of support mothers have banked on for eons.

Even the "Sexiest Man Alive" wasn't shy about household and family responsibilities he evidently shares with his wife by joking that his newly acquired title might give him a break from doing dishes and changing nappies.

In the twenty-first-century West, seismic cultural and economic changes raise new challenges for gender identity. Manhood initiation rites are missing, manhood has morphed into superficial and temporary rather than substantive qualities that have enduring significance, and gender roles are in flux. Women may be crossing gender barriers for education and careers. But men are transitioning too. Gender roles clearly delineated in previous generations (and still in many regions of the world) are up for grabs in the West. The world seems swallowed up in ambiguity. What is happening? And how will the church respond?

Evangelicals are not immune to these changes but in growing numbers (and not just millennials) are embracing them. In such a context, the church's message for men and women can seem outdated and irrelevant. Instead of offering men a message that accompanies them unbroken through every stage of life and holds up in the face of every shifting cultural current, the church's message for men seems inflexible and often ties their hands behind their backs instead of freeing them to embrace their lives and to do what needs to be done.

ROCKIN' ROLES

If the Gospel of Matthew were packaged like *People Magazine*, the hammer-wielding carpenter Joseph's face would grace the cover and not because of chiseled abs. Joseph would be featured because he represents a different kind of muscularity, one that defies his culture's expectations.

Joseph of Nazareth was a strong man, but his strength was used to serve God. All too often Joseph is overlooked, relegated to little more than a sidebar to the more important story of Mary and Jesus. If we are honest, he has the dubious distinction of being eclipsed by his wife and her daring "Yes!" to God. Every Christmas we unconsciously celebrate Joseph's manly humiliation on greeting cards that depict the holy family and in pageants where he blends into the background and can easily be mistaken for one of the shepherds.

But Joseph is not an incidental male in the larger story of redemption. He plays a strategic and indispensable role. The whole narrative would collapse were it not for this remarkable man. Joseph is key, and Matthew, for one, acknowledges his significance.

The first order of business is to establish Joseph's lineage. Not just any Jewish man will do for the role God is calling him to take. As we noted in the predicament the Albanian *burrneshas* faced, family lineage under patriarchy is patrilineal (i.e., it is traced through men). So in the ancient patriarchal Jewish world, Jesus' legal claim to the throne of David doesn't hinge on Mary, but on her husband, Joseph.[9] So before doing anything else, Matthew traces Jesus' lineage from Abraham through King David to Joseph. In case readers miss the point, the angel addresses Joseph as, "Joseph, son of David."[10]

Joseph's heritage is no trivial matter. Establishing Joseph's ancestry is crucial for Mary's son. This is the tipping point of human history, where everything changes forever. Joseph's lineage establishes the fact that the child to be born is the legitimate heir to the throne of King David. But much more is riding on the character and determination of Joseph. This reality comes into vivid focus when the little child of an ordinary couple from Nazareth is deemed a threat against King Herod, who mounts a massacre of baby boys in hopes of eliminating the boy king.

Underscoring Joseph's crucial role in events surrounding Jesus' birth and early years is the fact that unlike Mary and the shepherds, who each have a single encounter with the angels,

Joseph has four angelic visions. Through these dreams Joseph received vital directives that rescue Mary from the hazards faced by a pregnant single mother and that later keep the young Jesus safe from the powerful forces seeking to eliminate him.[11] Much of the story hinges on Joseph's obedience. But there is even more.

Often overlooked, yet central to Matthew's gospel, is the fact that on the opening pages Joseph embodies a brand of manhood that is alien in our fallen world where power, wealth, social status, primacy over women, and even physique are the gold standards for ranking men. Mary may give us a breathtaking example of the courage and self-sacrifice required of a young girl who follows Jesus, but Joseph is in every respect her match. He embraces a radical gospel brand of manhood that dismantles cultural and religious systems — both then and now — that falsely define what it means to be a man. He fills in more of the missing chapter. Even before Jesus is born, the kingdom of God touches down in Joseph's life. God has taken hold of the carpenter's heart, and he will not follow the herd. Joseph breaks from the pack.

Joseph's brief story sets the tone for the entire gospel and for Matthew's explanation of how the good news of Jesus changes everything. Joseph is Exhibit-A for kingdom living and gives us another powerful malestrom war story, for the kingdom of God is always at odds with malestrom currents that hold men captive to fallen cultural expectations and in the process cause men to lose themselves and forget who God created them to be.

Joseph's story contains a surprisingly relevant example of gender role reversal, for this hard-working carpenter closes up shop to get behind God's calling on his wife. Joseph deserves to be the patron saint of every man today who not only recognizes God's calling on his wife, but who fearlessly champions her as she pursues it and takes great pride in her accomplishments.

Joseph champions Mary in the thick of patriarchal traditions, which is even more remarkable. We diminish his courageous actions when we excise his story from the ancient cultural context that made his choices exceedingly revolutionary. Joseph didn't have the benefit of a men's support group to encourage him in his culturally groundbreaking efforts, although Matthew certainly gives him props. Instead of roundly criticizing or shaming Joseph for failing to "man up" in expected ways or relegating him to a supporting actor and a sidebar to the real story, the apostle shines the spotlight on Joseph's gospel-infused manhood and grants him the honor of opening the greatest story ever told.

AN UNCOMMON RIGHTEOUSNESS

Righteousness is a central theme in Matthew's gospel, and he begins that whole discussion with Joseph. Matthew contrasts two different types of righteousness that he has personally experienced: the righteousness of the Pharisees, which came down hard on him and shut him out, and the righteousness that Jesus embodied, which welcomed him and led him to a new beginning. Jesus contrasts his righteousness with that of the Pharisees and with shocking consequences: "Unless your righteousness surpasses that of the Pharisees and the teachers of the law, you will certainly not enter the kingdom of heaven."[12] Joseph's story makes righteousness a determinative factor in the crisis over Mary's pregnancy.

Joseph lived in a world where the Pharisees governed the prevailing notions of "righteousness." Theirs was a black-and-white determination of who's right and who's wrong, who's in and who's out, who's most pleasing to God and who's an outcast. How a person measured up determined how they were treated. For Pharisees righteousness was an exacting *external* standard—a system of outward practices, a religious yardstick against which they measured themselves and everyone else. It was, in fact, a self-righteousness that produced pride and invited intense scrutiny of others with the inevitable concomitant of harsh judgment on any violation. This kind of pharisaical righteousness left nothing but scorched souls in its wake. Even worse, it created religious vanity.

In view of the prevailing definition of righteousness in the ancient Jewish culture, Matthew's description of Joseph as "a righteous man"[13] should cause readers to shudder because "righteous" Jews are quick to pick up stones for violators of the Mosaic law. If we didn't already know how Mary's story turned out, this descriptor might very well be the death of Mary, considering how the Pharisees later drag a woman caught in adultery to Jesus with every intention of stoning her to death.

Under the circumstances Mary too was assumed to be an adulteress.

The fact that we have the full story in hand must not prevent us from pondering the awful peril Mary assumed when she willingly embraced God's mission to bear a son apart from Joseph and contemplated facing him. Bearing sons for Joseph was her mission as his wife, her life's work as a woman. That's how she expected her story to play out. Her betrothal to Joseph was legally fixed and was as fully binding as marriage—probably had been settled for most of her young life as these family arrangements were often made early. The fact that Mary and Joseph were not yet living under the same roof as husband and wife meant she hadn't yet reached (or was on the verge of reaching puberty) and could have been as young as twelve. So the actual marriage celebration and living together as husband and wife had not yet taken place.

There is only one way a young girl gets pregnant, and it is not because of some preposterous fairy tale of divine intervention. The Bible doesn't contain any record of some heart-to-heart conversation between Mary and Joseph or of her futile attempts to explain what really happened. Joseph may simply have discovered she was pregnant—which at some point becomes hard to hide. It had to be a terrible discovery for him. He knew for certain that she wasn't carrying his child.

According to patriarchy, Joseph's male honor is the main casualty here. Culturally speaking, what this means for Mary is straightforward. The only uncertainty is what form her punishment will take. As we noted in the chapter about Judah, vindication of male honor is a major factor in terrible violence against women, and patriarchy often gives men vigilante powers to do what they will with impunity. Even today there are those who believe a man has the right to beat his wife if she doesn't do what he says. Under Mosaic law, Mary had committed a capital offense.[14] If Joseph's righteousness conformed to the Pharisees' definition, Mary might well have faced the threat of an honor killing.

Some equate the label "righteous" to mean Joseph was acting out of "deep religious conviction"[15] and his "dedication to the Law."[16] They conclude that this religious righteousness curbed any inclination to shame her. Joseph certainly deserves high marks in this respect. But this definition doesn't explain Joseph.

KINGDOM RIGHTEOUSNESS IN ACTION

Neither the Old nor the New Testament regards true righteousness as a stand-alone concept that merely describes a person's standing before God. In the New Testament righteousness and justice are used interchangeably to translate the same Greek word, which underscores the unity between these two concepts. Even English translators of the New Testament don't always agree which of the two words to choose for a particular passage. But the connection is strong — the righteous person is also a just person. N. T. Wright captures this conceptual congruity when he describes the Sermon on the Mount as God's

> agenda for kingdom people ... the way in which Jesus wants to rule the world. He wants to do it *through* this sort of people — people, actually, just like himself. The Sermon on the Mount is a call to Jesus's followers to take up their

vocation as light to the world, as salt to the earth—in other words, as people through whom Jesus's kingdom vision is to become a reality. This is how to be the people through whom the victory of Jesus over the powers of sin and death is to be implemented in the wider world. (emphasis original)[17]

Righteousness is the active inevitable outworking of a person's restored relationship with God in just relationships with others. It is powerful kingdom energy that seeks expression in relationships and concrete action. Somewhere along the line, God took hold of Joseph's heart and transformed him into a truly righteous man. In the crisis before him, the first marriage was the union of his relationship with God and his relationship with Mary. It is all of a piece.

Jesus wasn't born yet. Joseph hadn't heard and probably didn't live to hear the Sermon on the Mount. He was an Old Testament Jew, so his understanding of righteousness came from Israel's history and from Old Testament teaching. The prophet Jeremiah conveyed an emphatic message to God's people on the subject of righteousness when he wrote:

This is what the LORD says:

> "Don't let the wise boast in their wisdom,
>   or the powerful boast in their power,
>   or the rich boast in their riches.
> But those who wish to boast
>   should boast in this alone:
>   that they truly know me and understand that I am the Lord
>   who demonstrates *unfailing love*
>   and who brings *justice* and *righteousness* to the earth,
> and that I delight in these things.
>   I, the LORD, have spoken!"[18]

In God's eyes, unfailing love (*hesed*), justice, and righteousness are a package deal. Jesus is the ultimate expression of all three and the one in whom the Father is "well pleased."[19] In

Jesus' life and death, he redefines, expands, and expresses all three. His righteousness provides the entire human race with hope. God delights when these words describe how his image bearers act toward others, for that is when they truly reflect him. These words call for sacrifice, forgiveness, and going the extra mile. This kind of righteousness puts the believer in a perpetual conflict of interest—even in relation to those who wrong us.

According to the Bible, justice at the human level isn't a top-down concept but is viewed from the perspective of those who live under the weight of injustice and whose cries God hears—the powerless, the oppressed, the widow, the orphan, the poor, and the foreigner. The view from the top of the human pyramid easily distorts justice. As one former American slave remarked in 1855: "Tisn't he who has stood and looked on, that can tell you what slavery is—tis he who has endured."[20]

This is the call of the gospel: to put the interests of others ahead of ourselves and to forgive, love, intervene, and bless. Righteous living violates the malestrom, every instinct of a fallen human heart, and earth-bound concepts of justice. Joseph doesn't think in fragments. He doesn't divorce righteousness from justice or from *hesed*. In Joseph's story, "righteousness and relationship [are] two sides of the same coin."[21]

Joseph's actions under duress demonstrate what righteousness looks like in a man whose culture pressures him to act one way but whose righteous heart leads him differently. His dilemma over Mary's out-of-wedlock pregnancy and apparent betrayal sets the context. Contrary to cultural expectations, Joseph makes choices that go against his own sense of honor and that will diminish him in the eyes of his community. But he plans to do it anyway.

Jesus introduces a whole new and utterly uncommon realm of righteous living when he preaches his Sermon on the Mount. Jesus expands the full range of meaning in this extraordinary righteousness when he sums up the entire law in response to the

question, "Of all the commandments, which is the most important?"[22] His answer points in two interlaced directions, "Love
the Lord your God with all your heart and with all your soul
and with all your mind and with all your strength," and "Love
your neighbor as yourself," adding, "There is no commandment
greater than these."[23]

The Sermon on the Mount merges the two—love of God
and love of neighbor. In fact, Jesus constantly weaves together
the implications of walking before God and how we care for
others on his behalf. In the Bible as a whole and according to
Jesus, loving God and loving one's neighbor are interlocking
concepts—permanently wedded together. This is true righteousness. You can't have one without the other.

A RADICALLY RIGHTEOUS MAN

The Christmas story is embedded in God's Greater Story,
and Joseph's role in the story involves a fierce battle with the
malestrom's firm grip on the pressure to "be a man" in the eyes
of his community. In a shame-based culture, it is difficult to comprehend the pressure Joseph must have felt. Everything hangs
by a slender thread as an unwed virgin conceives a child and a
deeply broken, dishonored man faces the biggest decision of his
life. But this is also where the kingdom of heaven touches down
on earth. Joseph is caught between the religious and cultural
status quo of what it takes to be a man in Israel and the claims
of heaven's radical righteous ethos on the decision he must make.

Marriage to Mary is out of the question, for as anyone in
Joseph's position would assume, she is carrying another man's
child. Yet, while still believing the worst about her, instead of
vindicating his honor by making her pay publicly for betraying
him, Joseph secretly plans to shield Mary from public humiliation (or worse) by divorcing her privately before two or three
witnesses. A radical righteousness indeed.

His contemporaries would consider this the worst sort of spinelessness—a classic case of wimping out. But Joseph was no milquetoast male. He was a man who at great cost to himself defiantly sought first the kingdom of God. The choice he made to consider Mary's interests ahead of himself took courage and prefigures the gospel. If we only knew this much of Joseph's story, we would have reason enough to admire him. But the story is only getting started, and God will ask a whole lot more of Joseph.

The angel's message in Joseph's first dream must have come as a double shock to Joseph—first by corroborating Mary's story and second by instructing him to marry her. Now, not only is he refusing to defend his honor, he is joining her in shame. But even this is not the last of the sacrifices Joseph will make. After Joseph takes Mary as his wife, he "shuts down his carpenter shop, gets behind Mary's calling, and adapts himself to his wife and God's calling on her life."[24] His whole life will be committed to making sure she succeeds in carrying out the mission God has entrusted to her. Even according to today's egalitarian standards, this is radical.

Muscles Joseph flexes in this story weren't for photo ops, creating a marketable celebrity image, or advancing his carpentry business. Nor was he flexing his manhood over Mary—expecting her to build her story around his, as his culture would demand. He has a different sense of manhood.

These are costly decisions for Joseph for they diminish his reputation in the community, turn his life upside down, and run his private agenda through a shredder. But he is every bit as resolute as Mary when she subordinated her public reputation to the private call of God and said, "Behold, the bondslave of the Lord; may it be done to me according to your word."[25] In these dramatic decisions, Joseph takes manhood to a whole new gospel level and foreshadows a new kingdom brand of righteousness.

Instead of the settled life they both envisioned, Joseph and

Mary face total upheaval, life-threatening danger, and life on the run. We prefer the dressed up version that shows up on Christmas cards and in Christmas carols. But this is anything but a pretty story. An edict from Caesar Augustus sends Joseph and a very pregnant Mary traveling to Bethlehem to register for Roman taxes. There, Mary delivers her royal baby in a smelly stable without even the most basic amenities. So far as we know, Joseph may have been her stand-in midwife, for they were far from the community of women who would have given her support.[26] Evidently they remained in Bethlehem, for they are still living there and Jesus is a young child when the Magi arrive. The Magi's inquiries in Jerusalem about the one "who has been born king of the Jews"[27] alerts King Herod to the birth of a rival king, a threat the king will not tolerate.

Joseph has more dreams and urgent divine instructions that force them to immigrate to Egypt during the remainder of Herod's reign and then to return to Israel after the king's death. But Herod's son Herod Archelaus isn't any safer, so yet another dream directs Joseph to Nazareth. After that, the gospel writers are silent about Jesus' childhood until he is twelve—a major year in a Jewish boy's life when he transitions from the care of his mother to work alongside his father and take up the family business. This significant transition was especially important for a firstborn son and a big event for the family's future. But for Joseph, this turning point brings one more disappointment that he must have felt deeply.

By then, Joseph and Mary no doubt had other children. Joseph and his family made their annual pilgrimage to Jerusalem for the Passover. Returning home, Joseph and Mary each must have assumed Jesus was traveling with the other or somewhere in the company with whom they were traveling. A whole day of travel elapsed before they compared notes and realized Jesus was missing. Any parent who has lost track of a child for even the briefest span of time will know something of the heart-stopping panic they lived with when for three full days they couldn't find him. Eventually, they found him in the temple among the teachers, listening, asking questions, and astonishing them with "his understanding and his answers."[28]

After three days of frantic anxiety and desperate searching, his mother's rebuke makes a lot of sense and actually sounds pretty restrained: "Why have you treated us like this?" Instead of responding like a chastened child, Jesus speaks words that ended what little was left of Joseph's original script. "Didn't you know I had to be in my Father's house?"[29] The thought may have crossed Joseph's mind, "But I am your father and you are not in my house." This is no dream, but the unexpected words of the young Jesus provide divine guidance for Joseph and reorient the carpenter yet again. The son he has raised as his own has a higher allegiance and won't be taking up his carpenter business. Like both Mary and Joseph, Jesus too had embraced the call of his Father in heaven and would take Joseph's righteous legacy to a whole new level. Joseph would have been proud of his son.

MISSING JOSEPH

It's understandable that Joseph goes missing from the lineup of male role models when his story takes place within the extraordinary events surrounding the birth of Jesus and his remarkable mother Mary. It's hardly an embarrassment to be eclipsed by Jesus and Mary. It may not rise to the level of being chosen to portray Mary in the Christmas pageant, but it is most certainly a badge of honor to be Joseph.

It's also possible that Joseph slips through the cracks because he fits into a similar category as Judge Deborah. Like Deborah, Joseph lived and acted in exceptional circumstances. Both Joseph and the role God called him to play in supporting and facilitating the mission God entrusted to Mary were a "special case," an exception to the rule. So we need to exercise caution before drawing theological conclusions about men from his story or making too much of him.

But for three reasons, I find it impossible to cast Joseph aside. The first reason is that Matthew calls Joseph righteous.[30] That description compels us to take him seriously. It means how he lived, what shaped his decisions, and the kinds of hard choices and sacrifices he made warrant careful examination and model the kind of life God calls his sons to live. It also means we can't dodge the fact that over and over again righteousness led him to violate his patriarchal culture's traditions of gender roles and how the Pharisees would have dealt with Mary's out-of-wedlock pregnancy.

The second reason I don't want to lose Joseph again is because whether we are male or female, we need his story. The stories of the men in this book have lots to say to and about men. Joseph's story gives the church fodder for a more thoughtful conversation about the challenges and changes men are facing today instead of assuming every change is a threat that must be resisted.

But ultimately none of the stories of the men in this book are exclusively man-stories. They belong to the whole church, and all of us need them. Joseph's story is a priceless gift when our own stories veer from the life script we carry around in our heads or that we inherit from our culture or from the church. Joseph is a man whose life script goes up in smoke the moment he discovers Mary is pregnant. From that point on, he must follow God into uncharted territory that raised eyebrows in his culture. Who of us doesn't need a story like his?

My late father preached a lot of incredible sermons that stick with me to this day. But perhaps the best sermon he ever preached took place in the privacy of my parents' home as he cared for my mother who was incapacitated after a surgery damaged her sciatic nerve. Whenever I went home for a visit and witnessed his selfless, loving care for her, I felt as if I was standing on sacred ground, watching the gospel in action as he sacrificed, poured himself out, and served her. He took her through daily exercises, managed her meds, cooked meals, washed dishes, shopped for groceries, ran errands, and accompanied her on countless doctor appointments. All the while he maintained his pastoral and preaching ministries and never uttered a word of complaint. When asked if this was too much, my dad always gently replied: "Do you hear me complaining?" It wasn't what he ever expected to be doing, but his heart was totally in it. Love has extraordinary powers.

We also need Joseph because he gives us a kingdom view of marriage that has profound implications for male/female relationships in any context. Joseph and Mary had a missional marriage. It was a true Blessed Alliance. Their marriage was an anomaly in their culture, but it was a blessing to the world. Their focus wasn't on roles or rules, cultural expectations, or power and authority. They focused solely on what God was calling *each* of them to do, and together they embraced God's mind-boggling purposes.

Joseph was a better man because he withstood the malestrom's currents, acknowledged Mary's special role, and got behind God's purposes for his wife. Joseph's very salvation depended on Mary fulfilling God's call on her. Both of them were making huge sacrifices, but that is how the gospel takes shape in the lives of the followers of Jesus. Righteousness drives the action. Joseph may have been losing ground in the eyes of his culture, but his actions carried cosmic significance. Every follower of Jesus is indebted to him. It is difficult to conceive of what might have happened to Mary without Joseph. One can only imagine the impact Joseph had on Jesus. We can be sure Joseph taught Jesus more than how to wield a hammer. Maybe Jesus learned more from Joseph by the sermon his stepfather was living. But even Jesus goes missing in some ways. We turn next to ask how Jesus battles the malestrom and how he shows men how to live as God's sons today.

DISCUSSION QUESTIONS

1. How are male/female roles reversing today—out of necessity, cultural and social factors, or simply by choice? Describe examples.

2. What does the perception of these changes as threats imply about the inadequacies of cultural and religious manhood definitions?

3. How does Joseph part ways with his culture in radical ways? At what personal cost to him? What frees him to do that?

4. How does the relational dimension of Jesus' righteousness/justice lead Joseph to embody a righteousness and justice that *exceed* standard definitions and contrast sharply with how we normally view these terms? What are the implications for us today?

5. How did Joseph battle the malestrom, and what does his story teach us about God's calling on his sons?

CHAPTER 8

THE MANHOOD OF JESUS

"Follow me!"
—Jesus of Nazareth

IN 1975 R. T. FRANCE, then Principal of Wycliffe Hall in Oxford, wrote a book about Jesus and submitted it to his publisher. They liked the book but not the title, *Jesus the Radical*. The new title, *The Man They Crucified*, was a compromise with his publisher, who balked at the description of Jesus as a radical. It was, they said, "open to misinterpretation."[1] In 1989, after the radical movements of the 60s and 70s calmed down and the word "radical" stopped sounding quite so radical, France rereleased the book with the title he wanted in the first place.

It was important to France to describe Jesus as a radical because the real Jesus was anything but conventional. He repeatedly ran afoul of cultural expectations and norms. He was a different kind of man—a very different kind of man. At every turn, he was at odds with prevailing Jewish standards. He was unmarried; he included women among the disciples who traveled with him; he touched lepers and the dead and allowed the touch of a menstruating woman; he kept company with criminals, traitors, and prostitutes; and he had an annoying tendency to violate Mosaic law—at least in the minds of the Pharisees. Jesus didn't go down easily in first-century Israel. In a word, Jesus was radical.

The best accounts we have of Jesus come from the four gospel

173

writers who give us something of a composite picture of Jesus by telling his story from different angles. Matthew writes as an eyewitness and a disciple who comes from the social margins. Mark is believed to have given his account based on the recollections and preaching of the apostle Peter. Luke, a physician, wasn't an eyewitness but, like an award-winning journalist, diligently researched his subject before putting pen to parchment. The apostle John wrote the fourth gospel from the unique close-up perspective of the self-described "apostle whom Jesus loved"[2] and who never seemed to relinquish his spot at the rabbi's elbow. Each story has its distinctive insights and perceptions of Jesus.

As a pastor's kid, I was introduced early to the practice of reading through the Bible every year. Admittedly, at first I didn't appreciate the value of four gospels and preferred following schedules that dispersed them among the other New Testament writings. Unfortunately, that approach tends to obscure the fact that the four gospels are not exact replicas but offer different vantage points on the life of Jesus. The very fact that there are four gospel accounts calls attention to the story of Jesus as the axis on which the rest of the Bible turns. These gospels make up nearly half (46 percent) of the entire New Testament. At the very least, that seems to place a rather large exclamation point next to Jesus' personal story—a story that carries central significance and that clearly cannot adequately be told by only one voice.

Even the four gospels together cannot tell the full story of Jesus. The apostle John admits that he has not captured every aspect of Jesus when he writes, "Jesus also did many other things. If they were all written down, I suppose the whole world could not contain the books that would be written."[3] So even what we get in the gospels is distilled down to what the authors felt were the critical essentials that readers need most.

Despite the fact that we don't possess an exhaustive record of the life of Jesus, gospel writers have managed to portray a mysteriously complex, unsettling, and paradigm-shattering Jesus, who is not always easy to understand. No matter how diligently we study these four gospels, how deeply we drill, how many gifted scholars and books we have to help us, how much true Christology thunders from pulpits, the stubborn fact remains that the quest to know and understand Jesus is always an unfinished and ongoing business.

AMBER ALERT

It is every parent's nightmare. After a family outing, the parents start to count noses and suddenly realize one of their children is missing. We immediately understand that Mary and Joseph must have been racked with worry. If the service had been available back then, they no doubt would have sent out an AMBER alert. They lost Jesus for three days, but I fear we lose Jesus again (without the panic) because of the way we read his story. An AMBER alert today might not be such a bad idea, at least to get us searching for him again.

In a way, Jesus goes missing from his own story. Historically, the church and our developing Christian theology have focused more on the signal events of the beginning and ending of the gospels — his birth, death, and resurrection, which were the center of early church controversies. Conclusions worked out in those controversies were codified in the historic creeds — The Apostles' and Nicene Creeds, for example. However, this had the unintentional effect of deemphasizing the middle part of his story — the life and ministry of Jesus. As N. T. Wright points out, "The great creeds, when they refer to Jesus, pass directly from his virgin birth to his suffering and death. The four gospels don't."[4] The Apostles' Creed, for example, affirms belief in Jesus who was "conceived by the Holy Spirit; born of the Virgin Mary" and goes straight from there to "he suffered under Pontius Pilate, was crucified, died and was buried ... on the third day he rose again from the dead."

Essential as it is for any creedal statement to affirm these crucial events, the gospel writers have much more to say about Jesus. The fact of the matter is that nearly 75 *percent* of what Matthew, Mark, Luke, and John think is important for us to know about Jesus happens between those three redemptive events of his life. As important as those key events are, it is also crucial to look as carefully at what Jesus said and did throughout his life. This raises important questions that are profoundly interconnected: How does that middle part of Jesus' story also inform our understanding of Jesus and his gospel? How does that stretch of Jesus' life shape *all* aspects of Christian theology and our understanding of the kingdom Jesus inaugurates? More specifically, how do his actions between his birth and death impact the church's theology of manhood?

When it comes to the church's gender discussion, I fear that Jesus goes missing here too. Of course, Jesus is not entirely left out, but he is not given the focal prominence in these discussions that rightfully belongs to him. The main interest seems to be in recruiting Jesus for one side or other of the debate: one side viewing his maleness as an affirmation of the priority of men over women or of maleness over femaleness, and the other seeing his countercultural interactions with women as carrying enduring significance and changing the role of women.

But Jesus is not a mere side point of argumentation. Jesus is himself central to our understanding of God's vision for his sons. Jesus is the prototype for what it means to be human as well as what it means to be male. He is our anthropological North Star.

When I prepared to write *Half the Church: Recapturing God's Global Vision for Women*, one of the ways I wanted to uncover more of the missing chapter was to explore feminine ideals in the Bible that teach us more about God's vision for his daughters without the distortions that came with the fall. I identified two brides: the Proverbs 31 woman (a text where a mother counsels her son on qualities to look for in a wife) and the Bride of Christ (who intriguingly also incorporates men and therefore presents an ideal for them as well).[5]

Jesus offers men the same opportunity. Jesus is the ideal man. Any conclusions we draw about what it means to be a man must begin with Jesus. This does not minimize in any way the fact that he was also God. But his identity as a human male should never get lost in his divinity. Jesus' maleness embodies God's vision for how his sons are to live and holds the key for combatting the malestrom.

What is more, it is also profoundly important for women that Jesus was male. His maleness was integral to the completion of his redemptive task, for it facilitated his ability to expose "the radical difference between God's ideal and the social structures of his day."[6] Let us not forget that in the ancient patriarchal culture, "only a male could have offered an authoritative critique of those power structures."[7] And Jesus' regard for women was truly earthshaking. His actions and relationships *as a man* vis-à-vis women carry more weight than we can possibly give them and prove even more culturally revolutionary than we generally acknowledge. "Jesus' association in public with women who were not his kin was a scandalous breech of decorum and a challenge to the gender boundaries of the first century."[8]

One only need imagine the very same Jesus walking around in today's Middle East and interacting with women as he freely did in first-century Palestine to get a sense of the jarring cultural impact he had on women and on how men viewed them. In contemporary patriarchal regions of the world, women cannot leave their homes without a male escort and are generally segregated from men in any public context. This current reality explains why R. T. France was right to call Jesus a radical. If Jesus is the perfect image bearer of God and our exemplar, the real question is: Are we radical enough?

So what do we learn from Jesus the man? What kind of manhood does Jesus define?

JESUS IN THE FLESH

Jesus was a man—a real living, breathing, Jewish male. We sometimes forget that basic fact. Early church fathers assumed that Jesus must have been the epitome of beauty. Augustine described Jesus as "beautiful God,... beautiful on earth, beautiful in the womb, beautiful in the hands of his parents,... beautiful in Heaven."[9] Consequently, in artistic depictions of Jesus over the last two millennia, he often is floating above ground with an impenetrable gaze, giving a limp wristed regal wave. The Jesus of our imaginations is Nordic, with pale skin, blue eyes, a long "Presbyterian" nose, and flowing locks of blond hair (or light brown in attempts to be more realistic) resting gently on his shoulders like some kind of proto-hippie. Of course, Jesus is portrayed as a six-footer, because surely he must have towered over everyone else.

But Jesus was a real man. The prophet Isaiah describes the Messiah as one with "no beauty ... nothing in his appearance that we should desire him."[10] Although New Testament writers who actually saw Jesus provide no physical description of him, forensic anthropologists and scholars have given a scientifically informed guess that brings a gritty reality to Jesus the man.[11] As a typical first-century Jewish male, Jesus probably had a broad peasant's face, dark olive skin, short curly hair,[12] a short-cropped beard, and a prominent nose. His height would have been about 5 feet, 1 inch, and his weight about 110 pounds. They think Jesus was short.

This makes Jesus about my size. It reminds me of what a teenager (who'd read my books) told her mom after meeting me at a conference. "I thought she'd be bigger."

Jesus would have worked outdoors under a blazing Middle-Eastern sun, so most likely even in his early thirties his skin was beginning to wrinkle. Although I hesitate to mention it to modern American readers (no nasty letters please), he probably did not smell like Calvin Klein. Jesus did not look like Brad Pitt or have the body of a Marvel superhero either; he looked more like a Jewish peasant who earned a living as a carpenter.

Jesus was a real boy too, and his parents would have had normal expectations of the traditional patriarchal trajectory his future should take, with primary focus on his father, Joseph. But Jesus plots a different course. When twelve-year-old Jesus went missing on the trip to Jerusalem, he was not lost. He was missing, but he emphatically denied that he was lost. This episode was no free-spirited adolescent grab for independence from parental control. Nor was Jesus engaging in some Freudian separation from his mother. If anything, Jesus' decision mirrored his mother who at about the same age made the same resolute choice. Both Mary and Joseph blazed the path Jesus chooses here, for both of them reached a point where what God asked of them trumped everything else.

Like every man-child born into the world, Jesus was God's image bearer from birth. But at this coming-of-age moment, Jesus embraces his calling to image God and drives a stake into the ground, so to speak, by declaring that from this point on his first allegiance is to his Father in heaven. Jesus' decisive choice to take up his Father's business came with a history that was firmly anchored in the Abrahamic covenant—to walk before God faithfully, rescue God's fallen image bearers, and be the agent of blessing to the nations. This is Jesus' mission. And so in his mind, he wasn't a lost boy, but an obedient son of his heavenly Father. In his first recorded words, Jesus embraces what Scot McKnight describes as "*the* fundamental human assignment" (emphasis original)[13]—the call to reflect God's image and to do his work in the world: "Why were you searching for me?... Didn't you know I had to be in my Father's house?"[14]

This is the first step any man takes toward actively fulfilling manhood as God defined it at creation. Image bearing is the sum and substance of manhood—the "all-or-nothing" point with

God that Abraham reached when he prepared to offer up his beloved Isaac, the watershed moment when Tamar forced Judah to take a long hard look at himself in the mirror, and Matthew's rapid response to the Rabbi's voice saying, "Follow me." It is a radical, utterly life-shaping moment.

MANHOOD IS THE *IMAGO DEI*

On March 13, 2013, Argentina's Jorge Mario Bergoglio was suddenly thrust into the public spotlight when the white smoke puffed out of the Vatican chimney and he began his papal reign as Pope Francis. The new pope—an unexpected selection—gained immediate notoriety and global admiration (even among Protestants) when he downsized from the palatial residence popes have historically occupied and moved into a modest two-bedroom apartment. This out-of-the-box former Argentine bishop prefers driving a Ford Focus to a chauffeured Mercedes and manages his own schedule.

But these changes, stunning though they may be, are mild compared to his unpredictable free and easy mingling with the public (unnerving to his bodyguards), his attentiveness to ordinary people, his relentless advocacy for the indigent and sick, and his forthright criticism of the prosperous. In contrast to his predecessors, he may be known for his humble, understated lifestyle, but this pope is also boldly outspoken and often veers from the expected pontifical script.

I don't know if *Rolling Stone Magazine* has ever shown interest in any previous popes, but Pope Francis certainly got their attention. According to their reporting, the pope's unvarnished criticisms that expose how prosperity "deadens" the world to the misery of the poor "resonate like a bomb." Reporter Mark Binelli remarked that Francis' actions "revealed obsessions to be more in line with the boss' son."[15]

But the cultural jolts that Pope Francis is causing by his

passion to follow Jesus are tame compared to how Jesus' obsession to be like his Father rocked the world during his lifetime or the powerful aftershocks he means for his followers to cause. He isn't merely waxing eloquent or distinguishing the spiritual realm from the physical when he says, "My kingdom is not of this world."[16] The coming of Jesus brought into sharp focus the dramatic difference between what passes as upright, acceptable (even religious) conduct and the kingdom of God he was inaugurating. He embodied a new and different way of being a male human that we lost in the fall. Jesus *is* the missing chapter.

Like the true image bearer he is, Jesus wanted nothing more than to "show the Father" to the world, and his actions and words constantly stunned the religious leaders, the throngs of people who gathered around him, and even his own disciples. He wasn't like the Messiah they expected—secretly amassing rebel troops and plotting the overthrow of Rome. His teachings (as in the Sermon on the Mount) were mind-boggling exposés that catapulted the Mosaic law from the letter to the spirit. The astonished crowds remarked to each other that they'd never heard or seen anything like him. A man's "obsession" to resemble his Father in heaven will inevitably send shock waves that disrupt cultural norms.

Image-bearer language saturates the gospel writer's stories of Jesus and also in how the apostles describe him later in letters to the churches. Once you start to see it, it's everywhere. The opening verses of John's gospel underscore the deity of Jesus—the Word who was "in the beginning ... with God ... and was God."[17] But John is also putting readers on notice that the one described here is God's image bearer par excellence. The apostle is emphatic, "No one has ever seen God, but the one and only Son, who is himself God and is in closest relationship with the Father, has made him known."[18] The writer to the Hebrews describes Jesus as "the exact representation" of God's being.[19] Paul describes Jesus as "being in the very form of God."[20]

Some of the most blatant image-bearer statements come straight from Jesus himself—claims that almost certainly bowled over anyone who heard him. "If you know me, you will know my Father as well. From now on you do know him and have seen him." This is not only a claim of deity, but of God revealed through a human person. In response to Philip's puzzled follow-up, "Lord, show us the Father," Jesus makes his assertion even more boldly: "Anyone who has seen me has seen the Father."[21]

Jesus the man identifies himself as the ultimate *imago dei*.

FOLLOW JESUS

When Jesus calls a man to follow him, he's actually repeating the Creator's high calling to represent God and to rule and subdue creation on his behalf. Cultural criteria of masculinity may get a lot of hype in discussions of manhood, but they fall woefully short of what God has in mind for his sons and often prove unattainable or unsustainable for a lot of men and boys. In contrast, Jesus' definition of manhood is every man's true identity and calling—his birthright. It encompasses everything about who he is and every second of his life.

The middle part of Jesus' story is rich with wisdom for how it looks when a man or boy actively pursues his calling to image God. So what does image bearing look like in the life of Jesus? Here are just a few observations that are especially significant.

First and foremost, Jesus devotes enormous attention to his own relationship with God. He is a man of prayer. That alone makes praying a man job. Jesus frequently breaks away from the crowds and his disciples to some isolated place to pray and commune with his Father. These were not perfunctory acts intended merely to set an example for his disciples. Jesus *needed* to pray. The few recorded prayers of Jesus that we have are not flowery soliloquies for the public to overhear or a to-do list for God, but signs of a real, open, honest, deeply personal, and at times desperate relationship. Jesus' prayers are earnest, even agonizing. They are filled with heartfelt outpourings for God's purposes in the world, expressions of utter dependence, realistic awareness of the threat of the Enemy, and honest, tortured wrestlings with his Father over the path that lay ahead. Something truly reorienting and utterly centering happens when a man falls to his knees to pray and align himself with God. Jesus leads men to that place.

But Jesus does more than pray.

Second, as one might expect, Jesus as *imago dei* moves from prayer to action—a self-conscious open awareness that he lives under the gaze of God. There is an intentionality about his words, his relationships, and his actions that comes from that mindset. "I do nothing on my own but speak just what the Father has taught me ... for I always do what pleases him."[22] Jesus lives out the Lord's Prayer.[23] The overarching goal of his life is to "hallow" his Father's name. "I honor my Father ... I obey his word."[24] In the middle part of his story, Jesus preaches the twin themes of the kingdom of heaven and the call for repentance (the need for a U-turn). "Jesus was *announcing that a whole new world was being born* and he was 'teaching' people how to live within that whole new world."[25] Manhood according to Jesus means a man lives knowing he's being watched, and nothing matters more than to be in step with his Father in heaven. That should completely revolutionize how a man lives.

Third, the manhood Jesus embodies inevitably means taking an oppositional stance against those malestrom forces that appeal to a man's pride and self-importance. Jesus endured a prolonged forty-day frontal assault from the evil one in the desert. Already weak from fasting, Jesus faced three temptations. This was not a practice drill or some charade Jesus conducted for our benefit. He endured a real full-on attack that, seen from the perspective of image bearing, reenacts the Enemy's successful assault in the garden of Eden. This was another attempt of the Enemy to drive a wedge between God and his image bearer by once again proposing enticing but illegitimate means (a shortcut) to legitimate ends, namely, God's purposes.

As God's image bearers, Adam and Eve were created to "be like God." But this was to be accomplished by means of a long-term relationship with God, not by eating forbidden fruit. Likewise, Jesus as the true Son of God was destined to reign over "all the kingdoms of the world," but not by gaining power through spectacular self-serving displays of his own powers or by bowing in worship to the Enemy. One can only imagine how potent the temptation was for Jesus to sidestep the painful, costly path of obedience to his Father. But Jesus' commitment to his Father holds firm. "The goal of obedience to the Father is accomplished, not by triumphant self-assertion, not by the exercise of power and authority, but paradoxically by the way of humility, service, and suffering."[26] This is the radical path of God's true sons—the path Adam abandoned but Jesus, the new Adam, pursues.

Jesus' habit of confronting and disturbing the peace of the powerful and prosperous—the religious and political rulers of the day—was not merely his rejection of the established power pyramid of his day, but a sober warning of the serious hazards of power and privilege in any place and at any level. "As one of Jesus' most popular one-liners says very clearly, 'the last will be first and the first last.' It is not good to be on the 'top.' "[27]

Jesus' inversion of the social pyramid—a malestrom social structure—is never more uncomfortably subversive than his rebuke of his disciples as they jockeyed for power and authority over each other (men over men!) in his coming kingdom. He doesn't simply rebuke them for fighting among themselves; he condemns how they are thinking. The prizing of power and authority over others may characterize the kingdoms of this world both large and minuscule. "Not so with you," he tells his disciples. "Instead, whoever wants to become great among you must be your servant, and whoever wants to be first must be your slave."[28] It is an astonishing inversion. A view of manhood that insists the top spot belongs to a male, in any context, is difficult to reconcile with Jesus' words. That's how hard it is to be the kind of man who follows Jesus.

This of course means that the masculinity Jesus exhibits is characterized by profound humility. One of Jesus' final acts was something only a slave would do—he knelt and washed his disciples' dirty feet. This is not like today's annual foot-washing services where everyone shows up with clean feet and a fresh pedicure. Peter's appalled and indignant refusal at the mere thought of Jesus washing his feet demonstrates just how completely unacceptable a thing this was for someone like Jesus to do. Jesus' reply wasn't to institute seasonal foot-washing ceremonies, but to explain this was how he expected them to live. I'm not sure the contemporary discussion of "servant-leadership" captures the full intent of what is going on here. Jesus is being far more radical than merely nuancing male leadership. Jesus is not telling his disciples to be kinder in their station at the top of the human pyramid. He is directing them to see themselves at the bottom and to conduct themselves accordingly—just as he has done for them. According to Jesus, the *imago dei* serves and cares for others. "I have set you an example that you should do as I have done for you."[29]

Jesus repeatedly pressed his disciples with an other-focused ministry of compassion and service to others. His view of manhood turns men outward to care for the needs of people. Like his Father in heaven, whose ears are open to the cries of the distressed, Jesus scoured the margins of society, acutely sensitized to the wounded, the oppressed, the forgotten, the shunned, and the broken. He fed the hungry, healed the sick, and redeployed the marginalized. Repeatedly he and his disciples are at odds, but he is unrelenting in leading those who follow him to respond compassionately and proactively to people's physical needs.

Things are not right in God's world—not then, not now. And it seemed his disciples were perpetually at odds with Jesus about the responsibilities that bearing God's image entails. Over and over again, Jesus showed them. When a large crowd of people followed Jesus into an isolated place and became hungry, the solution seemed obvious to his disciples: "Send the crowds away, so they can ... buy themselves some food." Instead, Jesus put the onus on his disciples saying, "*You* give them something to eat."[30] Jesus wasn't simply performing a big miracle; he was challenging his disciples to rethink their approach to people and to respond with care and compassion even beyond what they felt capable of doing.

His disciples "rebuked" those who brought little children to Jesus. Jesus welcomed little ones with open arms.[31] When blind Bartimaeus, a pitiful roadside beggar, heard Jesus leaving Jericho with his disciples and a large crowd, he cried after Jesus for mercy. "Many rebuked him" and essentially told him to shut up. But Jesus heard his cries, stopped in his tracks, and called for him to come.[32] When the Canaanite mother of a demon-possessed daughter refused to stop shouting out to Jesus for help, his disciples "urged" him to "send her away." Jesus engaged her and released her daughter.[33]

Jesus mirrors the Father, who hears the cries of the distressed. The whole story of the exodus centers on the fact that God hears the groans and cries of the Israelites and delivers them from slavery. Those same cries of distress are falling on the ears of God's image bearers and should, according to Jesus, elicit the same kind of urgent, compassionate response. His upside-down disciples are often disoriented, but gradually over time they begin to absorb his teaching and follow his example of manhood.

Finally, Jesus also frees men to express the full range of human emotions, not just in private prayer but in public. For starters, Jesus displayed love, compassion, sorrow, fear, courage, strength, vulnerability, anger, and dread. He wept publicly (actually sobbed aloud) in grief over the death of his friend Lazarus and wept openly over the resistance of Jerusalem.[34] Instead of men becoming pent-up emotional islands, Jesus gives men permission to be fully human, to admit that they struggle and are hurting, and to embrace the wholeness they were created to express as men. The fruit of the Spirit—"love, joy, peace, patience, kindness, goodness, faithfulness, gentleness and self-control"[35]—are not "chickified" qualities that need to be corrected with hyper-masculine traits, but the manly relational attributes of Jesus. The *imago dei's* interactions with people display God's heart for the world.

Already, Jesus' definition of manhood is a staggering proposition. Perhaps the most revealing aspect of Jesus' manhood, and a key place he counters the malestrom, is in his interactions with women.

JESUS AND THE *EZER*-WARRIORS

Nothing reveals Jesus' manhood like his countercultural relationships with women. Women weren't simply beneficiaries of his miracles and teaching, although that alone would be enough to change how men regard women today. The women Jesus knew were active facilitators and strong, indispensable allies in his mission. Most notably, his own mother was the first to give up everything to follow him. At the start of Jesus' story, everything was riding on the shoulders of one extraordinarily courageous young girl.

Jesus had deep friendships with women who were his beloved friends (the sisters Mary and Martha, and Mary Magdalene, for example). Women traveled with Jesus and his disciples, financially supported his ministry, and hosted his efforts.[36] Remarkably, women stood with him through the fiercest battle of all when his male disciples ran for cover. The women stuck with Jesus to the bitter end—witnessing the horrors of his execution and the finality of his burial, and sealing traumatic images in their minds they would never be able to erase. But they were indomitable. Before the sun rose the next Sunday morning (Roman soldiers notwithstanding), the women were back again at his tomb bringing spices to anoint his body, only to be gobsmacked by the astounding news that "he is risen!" It is difficult to imagine the emotional whiplash this caused or their flushed, excited faces as they fulfilled the rare privilege of breaking the news of Jesus' resurrection to his disbelieving disciples. The women were first to proclaim the gospel.

I grew up on these women's stories. But only as an adult did I return to look at them with new questions I was facing. In his miracles, his teaching, and his conversations, Jesus makes strong countercultural statements about the high value of women and girls in utter defiance of his patriarchal culture's way of seeing them. Mary of Bethany was one of the standouts for me. Jesus' interactions with this Mary takes the discussion of *ezer*-warrior to an entirely new level—well beyond making space at the table for women or "allowing" women to trespass into all-male territory.

Jesus' story includes three episodes involving this Mary; they are fragmented as no single gospel writer covers all three. But when I looked at Jesus' three encounters with Mary in toto, a whole new picture of Jesus emerged. In the first, Rabbi Jesus has a female student in his theological seminary as Mary sits at his feet to learn along with the men.[37] Jesus is teaching her the same deep theology he taught his male disciples. He doesn't just "permit" her to listen in either. When her actions are challenged and juxtaposed against the appropriate sphere for women, Jesus defends her choice in the strongest terms and recruits her sister Martha to join her.

Jesus and Mary meet a second time in the midst of a crisis. Mary is completely devastated and consumed by grief over the double loss of her beloved brother Lazarus and of Jesus' failure to come in time to prevent his death.[38] When Jesus seems most bewildering and disappointing, he takes her deeper and she learns to trust him, no matter how dark things get. In the final and strangest episode of all, the pieces of Mary's story come together when she anoints Jesus with expensive perfume.[39]

Like all of Jesus' disciples, Mary struggled to understand the upsetting things he was saying about laying down his life. His words conflicted with her messianic expectations too, especially with daily reminders of the Roman occupation. So when Mary invades an all-male feast intended to honor Jesus and anoints him with nard—a perfume the ancients used to pour on a corpse and an aroma everyone present recognized—her actions are intentional and infused with meaning that isn't lost on Jesus. She was his student. As she sat at his feet, he taught her the same things he told his male disciples about his approaching death. He had taken her to new depths of faith in the death of her brother and her disappointment with him.

In the midst of a party atmosphere, six days before the Passover that goes down in history as the Lord's Supper, with the looming battle ahead weighing heavily on Jesus and his male disciples in denial of what awaits him, Mary's anointing breaks his isolation and affirms the mission he's been telling his followers about for a long time. It's the only time anyone stood with him and said "Yes" to the cross and to the mission his Father has given him. In contrast, Peter's response was, "Never, Lord!... This shall never happen to you."[40] At Mary's anointing of Jesus, the disciples all chime in with Judas Iscariot to criticize her and point to the terrible waste of "expensive" perfume. In utter contrast, Jesus not only defends her actions, he interprets them. "When she poured this perfume on my body, she did it to prepare me for burial" adding, "She has done a beautiful thing to me."[41]

Jesus' relationships with women within an intensely patriarchal culture represent a paradigm shift for male/female relationships. Even for Jesus, "It is not good for the man to be alone." What is especially poignant is that Jesus' relationship with Mary sets a new tone. He values her theological insight and needs the resulting spiritual ministry this *ezer* offers. In this episode, Mary's ministry strengthens Jesus for the kingdom battle his Father calls him to fight. Stan Grenz puts a fine point on the radical implications of Jesus' encounter with the malestrom. "Coming to this earth as a man, Jesus liberated both men and women from their bondage to the social orders that violate God's intention for human life-in-community. Jesus freed males from their slavery to the role of domination that belongs to the fallen world, in order that they can be truly male."[42]

JESUS CONFRONTS THE MALESTROM

All along the way, Jesus is battling the malestrom on behalf of others. He parts company with his patriarchal culture when at the age of twelve, resisting patriarchal customs that obligate him as firstborn to center his identity and purpose in life on Joseph. Jesus embraces his *imago dei* identity, centers himself on his Father in heaven, and never looks back.

His life is a constant rejection of the pillars of patriarchy. He doesn't marry and produce sons to sustain the family for another generation. He ends up homeless. He subsists on the financial support of women, even asking a Samaritan woman for a drink of water. He rejects the patriarchal pyramid and turns it upside down. He recruits followers among ordinary and even marginalized men. His teaching upends the cultural value system by proclaiming the poor as blessed and teaching "the first will be last."

He deflects the devil's enticing offers of an easy way out and sets his face to follow his Father, no matter how difficult that path. Jesus refuses the world's power system and gains a kingdom by taking the place of a slave and laying down his life. He rejects the cultural divisions between male and female, draw-ing his male followers not only to see a different perspective of women but also to recognize their need of them. For starters, after Jesus' ascension, the four gospel writers cannot move forward without relying on eyewitness accounts from his mother, Mary Magdalene, and the other women.

The *imago dei* transcends patriarchal maleness and redefines manhood according to his gospel and the kingdom of God. God's vision for his sons is theirs at birth and can never be taken from them. Men who follow Jesus, who choose actively to pursue this calling, aren't taking an easy path. But the path they've chosen is well-worn. It bears the footprints of malestrom combatants who have gone before and leave a legacy worth inheriting: Abraham's brand of all-or-nothing faith; Judah's willing self-sacrifice despite his throbbing father wound; Barak's free and unrestrained celebration of the achievements and contributions of strong women; Boaz's willingness to listen, learn, and empower an Arab woman who lived on the hungry side of the law; Matthew's emergence from a dark and hopeless past to follow the Rabbi who offered hope and belonging; and Joseph, who put his whole life on hold to get behind God's calling on Mary.

All of these redemptive episodes anticipate Jesus, who calls men and boys to follow him into the indestructible calling they inherit at birth—a freedom and kingdom newness that is as old as creation, but utterly foreign to this fallen world.

This brings us full circle to ask again questions raised when we started: Does the gospel have anything better to offer men than a kinder, gentler patriarchy? Does God's vision for men fill the manhood void with a calling that covers the entire cultural spectrum and the complete life span of a man's life—no matter how long or how short that may be or how his story plays out? Does the church have a vision for men—a gospel of indestructible identity, hope, and purpose that will preach in the smoking ruins of Iraqi cities, in the slums of Nairobi, on the streets of Ferguson, Missouri, and to the utterly lost men of ISIS?

Discussion Questions

1. In what ways has Jesus gone missing? Why has this happened? What has this cost his church?

2. Why is the middle part of Jesus' story—his life as a man—central and foundational to any discussion of manhood?

3. Why was Jesus *not* lost when his parents couldn't find him? Why was that a turning point in his story? What was Jesus doing?

4. In what ways did Jesus, as the perfect *imago dei*, pursue his calling to image God?

5. How did Jesus battle the malestrom? How does his story radically transform the discussion of God's calling on his sons?

CHAPTER 9

LIBERATING MEN FROM THE MALESTROM

*"Hope is there within and among us, for we
are ordained of God to be people of hope.
It is there by virtue of our being in the
image of the promissory God."*
—Walter Brueggemann

IT'S NEVER A GOOD THING to be on the losing side of a war—even worse to end up a POW. In the case of one young German soldier, however, a three-year stint (1945–48) in a British prisoner of war camp was by far the best and worst thing that ever happened to him.

The worst part came not because he was mistreated but because he learned the truth. "As a young soldier in Hitler's army, Jürgen Moltmann (1926–) came to the dreadful realization that he had unwittingly served evil."[1] The horrible revelation came to him, as well as to other German POWs, when the British showed them photos of the Holocaust victims at Auschwitz and Belsen concentration camps. They had no idea. Despair and torment of soul descended. In Moltmann's words, "We were broken men, some of us fell sick during that time and died out of hopelessness."[2]

It is important for us to see this little known side of one of the worst chapters in human history. Even good men can lose themselves and without realizing what is happening. The malestrom is nothing if not devious.

Moltmann was liberated from the clutches of the malestrom when an American chaplain gave him a Bible and he began to read. He was deeply drawn to the Psalms, and as he read something inside of him changed. "I myself was gripped by a new hope which enabled me to survive. That hope was the hope of Christ."[3]

THE MARCH OF VIOLENCE

We are all familiar with the old adage that nothing is permanent except death and taxes. This adage should be amended to include violence—especially male violence. If the twentieth century has taught us anything, it is that violence is the defining characteristic of our era. That century saw five major wars that have claimed more than sixty million military deaths. If one takes into consideration the collateral damage, it has been estimated that about one hundred and eighty million people lost their lives in that blood-soaked century. More deaths resulted from the warfare in the twentieth century than all prior centuries combined. And these violent statistics do not include the twenty-first century, which got off to a murderous start with the terrorist attack of 9–11. As religion became virtually indistinguishable from political aims, we have witnessed the rise of suicidal terrorism. And the madness marches on.

By all accounts, the malestrom's currents are as fierce and relentless as ever, and the fall's effects on men are worse than we ever imagined.

The Middle East remains a hotspot with bombings, shootings, beheadings, and genocides. ISIS and other terrorist organizations are still on the move with visions in their sights of an Islamic caliphate under strict Sharia law. UN estimates of displaced minorities fleeing their pursuers and the mounting death tolls are mind-numbing, and "likely an understatement of the true scale of the slaughter."[4]

The market-driven underworld of human trafficking continues to thrive, fueled predominantly by male consumers of prostitution, pornography, and forced labor that depend on staggering numbers of men and boys "for hire." We sometimes forget that human trafficking victimizes both genders. This is not just a problem in "Third World countries" but is proliferating in and largely funded by the West. Tragically, we are also learning that sexual abuse is not confined to the Catholic Church, but involves trusted leaders within Protestant churches and ministry organizations who have horribly abused their powers.

Racial tensions have mushroomed in the US after two grand juries failed to indict police in separate incidents involving the deaths of unarmed black males — one in Ferguson, Missouri, and a second in New York City. Outraged protesters swarmed the streets of American cities in protest (and in some cases violent protest). Black Christian leaders are calling attention to systemic racism impacting men of color. Drew Hart sheds light on this problem when he points out that "racism is about one group having enough power to organize society by its categories ... in such a way that it advantages *most* of the dominant group's members at the expense of another group's welfare."[5] Protestors want to know if white Americans at the top of the social pyramid (including the church) will do "the hard work of listening and wrestling with another's perspective."[6]

If I ever questioned the destructive powers and ubiquitous workings of the malestrom, a single road trip would have eliminated those doubts. I was sobered by the exorbitant cost of male violence when the plane I took to Atlanta also transported the body of a fallen American marine. Waiting passengers rose to their feet, and the entire airport terminal came to a silent standstill as an honor guard of marines in full dress escorted the flag-draped coffin onto the plane. En route to the hotel, my cab driver revealed that he had been an Iraqi translator who served the US military during the Gulf Wars. But he too was grieving the violence, destruction, and corruption in his country and worried about loved ones who were still there.

My Iraqi cab driver/translator indicated that he had assisted US military interrogations of apprehended terrorists. What struck him most profoundly about these terrorist foot soldiers was that these young men were essentially hired guns. Poverty drove them to commit horrific violent acts for the equivalent of about fifty US dollars. "They don't have better options," he sighed.

I believe there is a better option.

THE GOSPEL OPTION

Jesus' gospel has a subversive power to reach behind enemy lines, draw men to Jesus, and free them from the grip of the malestrom. There is a biblical story about another man who, unlike Moltmann, was no "inadvertent" participant in evil who only "after the fact" discovered he had unknowingly supported evil. Saul of Tarsus (better known as the apostle Paul) was a ringleading religious terrorist, "breathing out murderous threats against the Lord's disciples"[7] and bent on destroying the nascent Christian church. An important part of Paul goes missing when we glide by his earlier incarnation as Saul of Tarsus—the Jewish zealot with blood on his hands—and only know him as the great apostle. Today, we have plenty of reference points for the kind of man Saul was. If the Internet had been available then, he undoubtedly would have posted videos of himself online delivering threatening terrorist messages with a balaclava covering his face. But Paul's cruel past is a vital clue to understanding him and to grasping the full impact of his letters to first-century churches.

As a devout Pharisee, Saul was fiercely committed to

maintaining Israel's distinctiveness and privilege as the chosen people of God—a status that excluded people from other nations. Already the Abrahamic covenant and Jewish circumcision had become symbols of national identity and exclusion instead of a calling to bless the nations. God's law was understood to draw an indelible boundary line between Israel and other nations. "An inevitable corollary was that the other nations, the Gentiles, were outside the scope of God's full favour, and unacceptable to him because of their lawlessness."[8] Saul, who later employs the word "zeal"[9] to describe his persecution of the church, is identifying his "wholehearted commitment to safeguard the privileges and prerogatives of Israel ... from any abuse or curtailment."[10]

Clearly, in Saul's mind, this commitment even warranted a "willingness to use force if necessary to maintain Israel's set-apartness from the other nations."[11] So when Jewish Christians began welcoming Gentiles into their midst, Saul detected an alarming trend that "broke down the protective barrier of the law and undermined Jewish set-apartness."[12] The breach must be stopped. So intense was his "zeal" for the Lord and the law that he stood at the forefront of efforts to wipe out this danger-ous corrupting new movement. He knew what he was doing and in his heart-of-hearts believed he was serving God.

Saul witnessed and gave his resolute approval to the bru-tal stoning execution of Stephen. Like a Taliban enforcer and with smoldering religious fervor, he relentlessly hunted down Christians. "Going from house to house, he dragged off both men and women and put them in prison."[13] His reputation as a terrorist who targeted Christians seems to have been wide-spread. Every Christian who faced the prospect of meeting him instantly recoiled in fear. No one knows, but it is doubtful that any believer would have entertained the wildly insane hope, much less prayed, that the gospel could ever transform a man like Saul. Christians were understandably terrified and tried to avoid him at all cost.

Saul proposed a strategy (which the high priest approved) for a terrorist campaign to expand his search-and-destroy activity into Syria. His goal was to work through local synagogues to track down and arrest any Christians—male or female—and haul them back to Jerusalem for trial. Indeed, it was while he was en route to carry out his violent mission in Damascus, the Syrian capital, that the gospel stopped him in his tracks. A blinding "light from heaven flashed around him," and he heard the voice of Jesus asking, "Saul, Saul, why do you persecute me?"[14]

It is ironic that the man so profoundly revolted and angered by the inclusion of Gentiles and who was leading the charge to wipe out this new "corrupting" movement is suddenly blinded and dependent on Christians and their willingness to accept and even protect him. There was enormous distrust among them at first, and for good reason: "they were all afraid of him, not believing he really was a disciple."[15]

Paul's powerful conversion story had a profound impact on Canon Andrew White, Vicar of St. George's Church in Baghdad, who has witnessed and still is witnessing the appalling suffering of believers in Iraq and in Jordan refugee camps. He's heard horrific firsthand stories of brutal executions that have taken the lives of so many of his flock—even of children who affirmed their love of "Yeshua" (Jesus) and refused to embrace Islam. In a Facebook post, he openly admitted, "At first I found it too hard to pray for the salvation of ISIS. They are just so evil. Then I realized they are just the kind of people that Jesus came to save. Pray for their salvation. Pray that Al Bagdadi [ISIS leader and mastermind] may see Jesus on his way to Damascus just like St Paul. Pray for their salvation."

Redemptive stories—like that of Jürgen Moltmann and Saul of Tarsus—give us a greater sense of the power of the gospel. The gospel of Jesus is bigger than we imagine and has a surprisingly long reach. Without a doubt it has the power to draw hopelessly lost men to Jesus. That gospel gives the church a message that restores men to their creation calling and invests them with a new identity, purpose, and sense of belonging.

THE GOSPEL VERSUS THE MALESTROM

Humanly speaking, no one would believe the radical reorientation that Jesus started when a devastated young German POW opened a Bible and began ~~pouring~~ *poring* over the Psalms. In Moltmann's despair he experienced the freeing power of forgiveness and a whole new sense of purpose. Through his personal anguish, he became a new and different kind of man.

Jürgen Moltmann went on to become widely known for his "theology of hope." "Although Moltmann did not actively mistreat Jews or participate in the 'final solution,' he was nevertheless acutely aware that, however inadvertently, he stood on the side of the oppressor in World War II."[16] That bitter reality, which Moltmann never got over, placed his study of Jesus, his cross, and resurrection squarely within the very raw and painful context of the worst of human suffering. The kind of hope he searched to understand and convey to others demanded honest wrestlings and asking hard questions. It meant refusing to settle for answers that can be extinguished when the darkness is overwhelming. His research ultimately brought the gospel's power of hope into the present. His "theology of hope has a here-and-now focus, which not only gives hope to the believer in the present, but energizes the believer to actively work to bring about the promised future."[17] That a theology of hope could emerge from such utter despair is a potent testament to the radical power of the gospel. It's the kind of sturdy hope the whole world needs.

Paul never got over God's grace to him either and always regarded himself as "the worst of sinners."[18] But Saul of Tarsus became Paul the apostle of Jesus. The apostle Paul is the unexpected Exhibit A of the fact that men and boys who follow Jesus are radical like the Jesus they follow. They defy the malestrom and embrace the freeing life-giving power of the gospel. They are not confined by patriarchy or any other cultural definition of what it means to be a man, but instead reclaim their Edenic call to image God.

The encounter with Jesus catapulted the former Pharisee into the epicenter of some of the world's biggest problems. Those problems have everything to do with people and the divisions among us that are fueled by power, race, gender, and class. Not only does his story infuse hope for men who have fallen prey to the malestrom—including the likes of terrorists, traffickers, abusers, men of violence, extortionists, and others the world will not forgive; his story also illustrates the radical reorientation of every man who follows Jesus' embrace.

Jesus' gospel shoves Paul across *the racial divide* between Jew and Gentile—a dividing wall the gospel shatters with the blunt force of a wrecking ball. It's difficult to imagine this was easy for Paul, a Pharisee whose father was also a Pharisee.[19] It meant going against everything he'd ever known and believed. And Jesus isn't asking Paul to make a slight shift in his thinking with respect to Gentiles or merely to adjust to the fact that God loves Gentiles too. Jesus appoints Paul to be the apostle to the Gentiles—to become the very bridge over which countless Gentiles will travel to follow Jesus. The irony is hard to absorb, but Jesus chose Paul to be his "chosen instrument to proclaim [his] name before the Gentiles and their kings."[20]

This call goes beyond simply welcoming Gentiles to love, nurture, pastor, fellowship, and partner with them in spreading the gospel to the nations. The old zeal of Saul is not cast out, but is redeemed and redirected in Paul who will embrace the Gentiles as wholeheartedly as he once persecuted Christians. He even goes beyond that to sacrifice and suffer so that the good news of Jesus can thrive among the people he once hated but now loves. Paul becomes a new and different kind of man for whom racial differences are no longer a source of conflict.

Jesus' gospel also pushes Paul across *the gender divide* by bringing strong *ezer*-warriors into his life—women he will need and depend on as coworkers and fellow-sufferers for the gospel. Many were Gentile women, which makes it all the more astonishing that this should ever happen. Through his friendships and collaboration with Gentile women, Paul crosses two cultural divides at once—race and gender. Paul has not only shed his Pharisaism, but also first-century patriarchal views of women. From accounts about Paul and the content in his letters, it is clear that Paul regarded these women with deep affection and admiration. He credits and depends on them as indispensable allies in his ministry (which is how God designed for things to work between male and female in the beginning).

There was Lydia,[21] the first believer and leader in the first church plant in Europe. He identifies Euodia and Syntyche[22] as fellow-laborers in Philippi, two indispensable kingdom *ezer*-warriors who "contended at [his] side in the cause of the gospel." At the end of his letter to the Romans, he gives a long list that includes a number of faithful women. Phoebe[23] is mentioned as a deacon and the envoy he entrusted with his letter to the church in Rome. He expresses affection and indebtedness for Priscilla,[24] the gifted teacher and his fellow-worker who risked her life for him. His respect is obvious for Junia,[25] an outstanding apostle who was imprisoned with Paul. He names Persis[26] as his "dear friend" who "worked very hard in the Lord," and Rufus' mother,[27] who was "a mother" to Paul too. Paul wasn't merely "including" women. He relied on their support, encouragement, and partnership in the gospel. Paul becomes a new and different kind of man, for whom patriarchy is no longer the obligatory social structure.

Before it's all over, Paul, as an old man, will shatter yet one more impenetrable barrier—*the socio-economic class divide*. He affectionately describes a runaway Gentile slave he met in prison as "my son, Onesimus" and "my very heart."[28] When

Paul sends Onesimus back to his Christian master, Paul pleads not only for the life of Onesimus, but drops hard-to-ignore hints that Philemon should free his former slave who, Paul argues, is now "better than a slave"[29] to Philemon. He is "a dear brother."[30] Paul has become a new and different kind of man, who sees other men as his brothers and not as any culture ranks them.

Paul rejects the social structures of ancient patriarchy and embodies his own radical countercultural words—that in Christ there is "neither Jew nor Gentile, neither slave nor free, neither male nor female, for you are all one in Christ Jesus."[31] Jesus may have been short, but he has undone the malestrom and overthrown patriarchy.

The Liberating Gospel of Jesus

The final chapter of a book is supposed to bring the subject to a conclusion. But any sense of closure to the subjects raised in this book evades me. Instead, the concerns that prompted me to write this book in the first place have only deepened as I have researched and learned more about the global crisis facing men and boys that started at the fall. The sense of urgency I felt when I started this project has only grown stronger as I watch the news, listen to men's stories, and simply see the look of recognition on their faces when I talk about the malestrom and what it's doing to men and boys. They've already met the malestrom.

At the same time, from the beginning this project has been infused with hope that for me has only burned brighter. I knew going in that hope would have the last word. But a topic like the malestrom doesn't lend itself to tidy conclusions. It cannot be contained in an entire book, much less in a few closing remarks. And although God has provided what we need to combat the malestrom, he doesn't offer simple formulas or a triumphalist approach. Instead, he arms us with an unrivaled global vision for his sons, some bracing examples of men who battled the malestrom and lived to tell the story, the perfect *imago dei* in Jesus, and his potent gospel powered by his Holy Spirit—and calls us to "continue to work out your salvation with fear and trembling,"[32] knowing he is with us in the battle.

As I reach the end of this literary journey, I must admit I have more questions than answers, and those questions deeply trouble me. I have barely scratched the surface of this enormous topic and its many knotty implications. To do full justice would require a tome or two. There remains much more work to do— to understand more fully what men and boys are facing in the twenty-first-century malestrom-battered world and to learn more about God's vision, the implications of the gospel, and the radical *imago dei* example Jesus sets for us.

The malestrom shows no sign of abating. It will be with us wreaking havoc in men's lives until Jesus comes. Every day, men and boys all over the world are being swept into the vortex by its currents. The malestrom poses a real and perpetual threat to every man and boy that we must not minimize and that we in good conscience cannot ignore.

Cultural definitions of manhood and rites of passage are not the answer. Historically the reigning definition has been patriarchy, although even patriarchy isn't a monolith, but a broad continuum of definitions ranging from the fanatical to kinder, gentler versions, none of which reflect the gospel or God's vision for his sons.

The gospel of Jesus liberates men from that continuum and the downward drag of the malestrom. "The truth will set you free,"[33] Jesus declares. Although the fall has deeply impacted males, hence the designation *male*-strom, the Bible gives us compelling examples of men who have broken free from the malestrom and emerge from the watery depths of the battle as changed men who reflect the newness Jesus brings.

Jesus was on a mission to restore the world God created and

loves deeply. He didn't come to make slight adjustments to the way things work in a fallen world. It was not his intention to offer men a kinder, gentler patriarchy. His mission was to turn this fallen world right side up. The men whose stories we have considered demonstrate a robust countercultural way of life. To bear God's image inevitably means going against the cultural grain.

But image bearing comes with kingdom responsibilities. Every man's first and primary calling is to know the God whose image he bears, to see the world through God's eyes, and to care for it on his behalf. It means the hard work of rebuilding that strategic Blessed Alliance between men and women falls on all of us. It is still "not good for the man to be alone." It means what's happening in God's world—the suffering, poverty, injustice—is our business as bearers of God's image. The task he entrusts to his sons (and daughters) is to join him in bringing God's kingdom on earth as it is in heaven.

And we have the gospel power of Jesus, the perfect *imago dei*, who is the missing chapter. Jesus is generously indiscriminate with his call to "Follow me!" He is actively reaching behind enemy lines where men seem most hopeless, but where his gospel brings hope and redeploys men for his kingdom. Jesus' gospel liberates men from the strictures of patriarchy and the powers of the malestrom. It restores them to their true calling as God's sons. And when the gospel gets hold of a man, the world will know that Jesus has come and that his kingdom is not of this world.

The only thing more tragic in all of this is for the church to remain silent in the face of the malestrom's challenges or to fail to "man up" and challenge our own theology of manhood with the pressing twenty-first-century realities confronting men and boys globally. Jesus calls his church to reclaim her prophetic voice and to show the world by our own embrace of his vision, the gospel, and one another that Jesus has come and that his kingdom is not of this world.

We belong in this fight. I pray that a door has been cracked open for a deeper, more robust discussion of the twenty-first-century issues facing men and how the Bible empowers men to resist the malestrom. The way forward is challenging. The problems are complex, and we have only begun to grasp the remedies God provides. But we are not walking into the darkness, for Jesus knows the way and is still saying, "Follow me!"

DISCUSSION QUESTIONS

1. What do the stories of Saul of Tarsus and Jürgen Moltmann have in common?

2. How did the gospel rescue both of them from the malestrom and put the hope and power of Jesus' gospel on display?

3. What radical changes did Jesus' gospel bring to both men's lives?

4. How does Jesus' gospel raise the bar for men, invest them with more dignity and meaning, and ask more of them than any cultural definition of manhood?

5. How big is God's heart for his sons—no matter how hopeless and lost they may be? How can the church share God's heart for them too? What must the church do to speak prophetically into this global crisis with a message of hope and purpose that can withstand the malestrom's strongest currents?

NOTES

INTRODUCTION: THE MALESTROM

1. Edgar Allan Poe, "A Descent into the Maelstrom," in *Edgar Allan Poe: Complete Tales and Poems* (Edison, NJ: Castle, 2002), 57.
2. David D. Gilmore, *Manhood in the Making—Cultural Concepts of Masculinity* (New Haven, CT: Yale University Press, 1990), 49.
3. Nicki Lisa Cole, "Full Transcript of Emma Watson's Speech on Gender Equality at the UN," http://sociology.about.com/od/Current-Events -in-Sociological-Context/fl/Full-Transcript-of-Emma-Watsons-Speech -on-Gender-Equality-at-the-UN.htm.
4. US Census Bureau; American Community Survey, 2013 American Community Survey 1-Year Estimates, Table B01003; generated by Amy Lauger; using American FactFinder; <http://factfinder2.census.gov>; (27 September 2014). NYC population was estimated at 8,405,837.
5. Congressional Briefing in April 2012, Dr. Howard Spivak, Director of the Division of Violence Prevention.
6. Stephen B. Boyd, *The Men We Long to Be: Beyond Domination to a New Christian Understanding of Manhood* (New York: HarperSanFrancisco, 1995), 85.
7. Carolyn Custis James, *Half the Church: Recapturing God's Global Vision for Women* (Grand Rapids: Zondervan, 2011), 37.
8. Gilmore, *Manhood in the Making*, 1.
9. E. Anthony Rotundo, *American Manhood: Transformations in Masculinity from the Revolution to the Modern Era* (New York: Basic Books, 1993), 1.
10. Gilmore, *Manhood in the Making*, 222.
11. Ibid., 223.
12. Rotundo, *American Manhood*, 3.
13. Susan Faludi, *Stiffed: The Betrayal of the American Man* (New York: William Morrow and Company, Inc., 1999), 14–15.
14. See www.npr.org/2014/06/23/323966448/the-new-american-man -doesnt-look-like-his-father.
15. Gilmore, *Manhood in the Making*, 11.

16. Ibid., 152.

17. Kay S. Hymowitz, *Manning Up: How the Rise of Women Has Turned Men into Boys* (New York: Basic Books, 2012), 171–72, 181–87.

18. Hanna Rosin, *The End of Men—and The Rise of Women* (New York: Riverhead, 2012), 5.

19. John L. Esposito, "The Challenges in Defeating ISIS," *TheWorldPost/ Huffington Post*, August 27, 2014, www.huffingtonpost.com/john-l -esposito/the-challenges-in-defeati_b_5722118.html.

20. Paul Brandeis Raushenbush, "Isis and the Crisis of Meaning," *Huffington Post*, August 28, 2014, www.huffingtonpost.com/paul -raushenbush/isis-and-the-crisis-of-meaning_b_5730284.html.

21. "Patriarchy," https://www.princeton.edu/~achaney/tmve/wiki100k /docs/Patriarchy.html.

22. "Egalitarianism must always lead to an eventual denial of the gospel" (John Piper and Wayne Grudem, *Recovering Biblical Manhood and Womanhood* [Wheaton, IL: Crossway, 2006], xi).

23. In *Lost Women of the Bible: The Women We Thought We Knew* (Grand Rapids: Zondervan, 2005), I coined the expression "Blessed Alliance," based on God blessing his male and female image bearers and commissioning them to do his work in the world together (cf. Gen 1:27–28). This alliance is not confined to marriage, but encompasses all male/female relations and is ultimately to be reflected in the church as the body of Christ. It is developed further in *The Gospel of Ruth: Loving God Enough to Break the Rules* (Grand Rapids: Zondervan, 2008), and *Half the Church: Recapturing God's Global Vision for Women* (Grand Rapids: Zondervan, 2011) and is discussed in subsequent chapters of this book.

24. John 18:36.

25. For further reading, see Carolyn Custis James, *When Life and Beliefs Collide* (Grand Rapids: Zondervan, 2000), *Lost Women of the Bible: The Women We Thought We Knew* (2005), *The Gospel of Ruth: Loving God Enough to Break the Rules* (2008), and *Half the Church: Recapturing God's Global Vision for Women* (2011).

26. The term *ezer*-warrior may be unfamiliar to some readers. It is based on the powerful military Hebrew word *ezer* that is used most often in the Old Testament to refer to Yahweh as the *ezer* (helper) of his people. God uses it twice in Genesis 2:18 and 20 to describe the female (*all* females, not exclusively wives). I have written extensively about the *ezer* in my previous books, *Lost Women of the Bible* (Grand Rapids: Zondervan, 2005) and *Half the Church* (Grand Rapids: Zondervan, 2011). *Ezer* is fully explained in the next chapter, "The Genesis of the Malestrom."

27. Walter Brueggemann, *Genesis*, ed. James Luther Mays, Interpretation: A Bible Commentary for Teaching and Preaching (Louisville, KY: Westminster John Knox, 2010), 5.

Chapter 1: The Genesis of the Malestrom

1. See www.desiringgod.org/biographies/the-frank-and-manly-mr-ryle -the-value-of-a-masculine-ministry.
2. Jan H. F. Meyer and Ray Land, "Threshold Concepts and Troublesome Knowledge—Linkages to Ways of Thinking and Practising," in *Improving Student Learning—Theory and Practice Ten Years On*, ed. C. Rust (Oxford: Oxford Center for Staff and Learning Development, 2003), 412–24.
3. Brueggemann, *Genesis*, 137.
4. Genesis 3:16b.
5. The Hebrew term *'adam* is translated "human beings" because when it is used with the definite article "the" (as it is here), it is not referring to males, but generically to *human beings*. Some recent English translations have insisted on perpetuating the archaic translation, "man." But that is misleading and actually makes "nonsense of the last clause of verse 27" that further defines the meaning of the terms as including "male and female." Robert Alter, *Genesis—Translation and Commentary* (New York: Norton, 1996), 9.
6. Genesis 1:26–27, TNIV (emphasis added).
7. John M. Frame, "Men and Women in the Image of God," in *Recovering Biblical Manhood and Womanhood: A Response to Evangelical Feminism*, ed. John Piper and Wayne Grudem (Wheaton, IL: Crossway Books, 1991), 225–32.
8. James, *Half the Church*, 52–53.
9. Genesis 5:3 (emphasis added).
10. Hansi Lo Wang, "To Model Manhood, Immigrant Dads Draw From Two Worlds" (NPR, *All Things Considered*, "CodeSwitch—Frontiers of Race, Culture and Ethnicity"), September 1, 2014, www.npr .org/blogs/codeswitch/2014/09/01/343984726/to-model-manhood -immigrant-dads draw-from-two-worlds.
11. Genesis 3:8.
12. Hebrews 1:3 (emphasis added).
13. John 14:9b.
14. Mae Elise Cannon, Lisa Sharon Harper, Troy Jackson, and Soong-Chan Rah, *Forgive Us: Confessions of a Compromised Faith* (Grand Rapids: Zondervan, 2014), 197.
15. Genesis 2:18 (emphasis added).
16. Genesis 2:24.

17. Brueggemann, *Genesis*, 45.

18. Genesis 2:15.

19. Genesis 3:24.

20. Alter, *Genesis*, 9.

21. See "Eve—A Forgotten Legacy," in James, *Lost Women of the Bible*, 27–45, and "The *Ezer* Unbound," in idem, *Half the Church*, 99–118.

22. Exodus 18:4; Deuteronomy 33:7, 26, 29; Psalms 20:2; 33:20; 70:5; 89:19 (translated "strength" in the NIV); 115:9, 10, 11; 121:1–2; 124:8; 146:5; Hosea 13:9.

23. Names like Eli-*ezer*, Abi-*ezer*, and just plain *Ezer* appear in the Bible. Even in recent history, evidence is strong that the name *Ezer* still carries a lot of weight. Israel's seventh president was *Ezer* Weizman (1924–2005). He was an Israeli military hero who built an international reputation as a fighter pilot, commander of the Israeli Air Force, and a world leader involved in Middle East peace negotiations.

24. Gerhard von Rad, *Old Testament Theology: The Theology of Israel's Historic Traditions* (New York: Harper & Row, 1962), 1:149–50.

25. Boyd, *The Men We Long to Be*, 118.

26. See R. Laird Harris, Gleason L. Archer Jr., and Bruce K. Waltke, eds., *Theological Wordbook of the Old Testament* (Chicago: Moody Press, 1980), 2:768: "God created woman by taking 'a rib' from Adam while he was in a very deep sleep. Conceivably this means that God took a good portion of Adam's side, since the man considers the woman to be 'bone of his bones' and flesh of his flesh (Gen 2:21ff). This picture describes the intimacy between man and woman as they stand equal before God."

27. Genesis 2:23.

28. Genesis 1:27.

29. Genesis 1:31.

30. Andy Crouch, *Playing God: Redeeming the Gift of Power* (Downers Grove, IL: InterVarsity Press, 2013), 97.

31. Some have argued, based on ancient practices, that *naming* is an act of authority and dominion, so that Adam's naming of the animals and later naming the woman establishes male authority. But this argument is difficult to sustain in support of male authority over females, for in Genesis alone the order is reversed. Beginning in Genesis 4:25, women (Eve, and Israel's matriarchs, Leah, and Rachel) name their sons. Even more problematic to this line of argument is when the Egyptian slave girl Hagar names God *El Roi*, "the God who sees me" (Genesis 16:13). Victor Hamilton believes "it is stretching the point to suggest that in naming the animals man exercises sovereignty over them. For that to be clear, one would need a parallel to the 'subdue' and 'have dominion over' of Ch. 1. In naming the animals, man exercises a God-given

initiative.... In acting as a name-giver, the man exhibits a quality of discernment" (Victor Hamilton, *The Book of Genesis Chapters 1–17*, New International Commentary on the Old Testament [Grand Rapids: Eerdmans, 1990], 177).

32. 1 Timothy 2:14.

33. Genesis 3:12.

34. Genesis 3:16.

35. Lilian Calles Barger, *Eve's Revenge: Women and a Spirituality of the Body* (Grand Rapids: Brazos, 2003), 138.

36. Ibid.

37. Boyd, *The Men We Long to Be*, 86.

CHAPTER 2: PATRIARCHY MATTERS

1. Michael Paterniti, "The Mountains Where Women Live as Men," *GQ Magazine* (March 2014), 198; www.gq.com/news-politics /newsmakers/201403/burrnesha-albanian-women-living-as-men.

2. Numbers 26:33; 27:1–11; 36:1–12.

3. Patrilineal practices mean such things as property, wealth, and the family name were passed from father to son and down through the male line.

4. Paterniti, "The Mountains Where Women Live as Men," 198.

5. Ibid., only in online copy: www.gq.com/news-politics/newsmakers /201403/burrnesha-albanian-women-living-as-men.

6. Kanun is a medieval canon of traditional Albanian laws.

7. Paterniti, "The Mountains Where Women Live as Men," 200.

8. Christian Piatt, "Foreword," in *Father Factor: American Christian Men on Fatherhood and Faith*, ed. R. Anderson Campbell (Ashland, OR: White Cloud, 2014), x.

9. Genesis 12:1.

10. Brueggemann, *Genesis*, 146–47.

11. Gordon J. Wenham, *Genesis 16–50*, Word Biblical Commentary (Waco, TX: Word, 1994), 16.

12. Genesis 17:5–6 (emphasis added).

13. Brueggemann, *Genesis*, 209–10.

14. Genesis 12:5b, 16.

15. Genesis 17:12–13, 27.

16. James, *Lost Women of the Bible*, 70. Genesis 12:19 (emphasis added).

17. Genesis 2:24 (emphasis added).

18. David Fitch, "Beyond Egalitarianism and Complementarianism: The Kingdom Call for Women in Ministry," *Missio Alliance* (July 17, 2014); see www.missioalliance.org/beyond-egalitarianism-and -complementarianism-the-kingdom-call-for-women-in-ministry/.

19. Genesis 17.
20. Hamilton, *The Book of Genesis Chapters 1–17*, 468.
21. Genesis 17:1.
22. Genesis 34:24–29.
23. Hamilton, *The Book of Genesis Chapters 1–17*, 470.
24. Hebrews 11:10, 13, 16.

CHAPTER 3: THE FATHER WOUND

1. Richard Rohr, *From Wild Man to Wise Man: Reflections on Male Spirituality* (Cincinnati, OH: St. Anthony Messenger, 2005), 77.
2. Wes Yoder, *Bond of Brothers: Connecting with Other Men beyond Work, Weather, and Sports* (Grand Rapids: Zondervan, 2010), 69.
3. Genesis 46:7.
4. Genesis 30:21.
5. Genesis 34.
6. Bruce K. Waltke, *Genesis* (Grand Rapids: Zondervan, 2001), 468.
7. Matthew 20:16.
8. Robert Alter, *The Art of Biblical Narrative* (New York: Basic Books, 2011), 5.
9. Genesis 25:23.
10. Brueggemann, *Genesis*, 209.
11. From *Lord of the Rings*.
12. Genesis 29:26.
13. Genesis 29:32–35; 30:17–20.
14. Genesis 29:31.
15. Genesis 37:3 (emphasis added).
16. Waltke, *Genesis*, 498.
17. Ibid.
18. "In the earliest times of the Bible [cisterns] were used to store water. They were usually pear shaped, and 15 to 20 feet deep, and the actual opening was only 2 to 3 feet. There was usually a stone cover. Cisterns were either large or small, large enough to store water for the community, or small and privately owned. Cisterns were like wells of water, which could be hoisted up with ropes and a bucket." "Ancient Cisterns," from www.bible-history.com/biblestudy/cisterns.html.
19. Alter, *The Art of Biblical Narrative*, 2.
20. Gordon J. Wenham, *Genesis 16–50*, ed. David A. Hubbard and Glenn W. Barker, Word Biblical Commentary (Dallas: Word, 1994), 364.
21. Richard Rohr, *Falling Upward: A Spirituality for the Two Halves of Life* (San Francisco, California: Jossey-Bass, 2011), 158–59.
22. Genesis 35:22; much later, when King David's son Absalom pitched a tent on the palace roof and slept with his father's concubines, it was

a public act of defiance, making Absalom "a stench in [his] father's nostrils" (2 Samuel 16:21–22, NIV 1984).

23. Genesis 34:30 (NIV 1984).
24. Genesis 38:7 and 10.
25. "If [a brother] dies without a son, his widow must not marry outside the family. Her husband's brother shall … marry her and fulfill the duty of a brother-in-law to her. The first son she bears shall carry on the name of the dead brother so the name of the dead brother will not be blotted out from Israel" (Deuteronomy 25:5–6).
26. The label "john" is the slang expression used to refer to men who solicit the services of prostitutes and is thought perhaps to have resulted from so many men seeking anonymity by saying their name was "John."
27. Tamar is named with the deepest respect in the blessing pronounced on the marriage of Ruth and Boaz (Ruth 4:12); King David and his son Absalom each name a daughter after her (2 Samuel 13:1; 14:27); and she is included in Matthew's genealogy as an ancestress of Jesus, whose sense of family honor led her to rescue the royal line of the Messiah (Matthew 1:3).
28. Wenham, *Genesis 16–50*, 362; Victor P. Hamilton, *The Book of Genesis Chapters 18–50*, ed. R. K. Harrison and Robert L. Hubbard Jr., The New International Commentary on the Old Testament (Grand Rapids: Eerdmans, 1995), 446.
29. Genesis 44:18–34, NLT (emphasis added).
30. Genesis 44:20.
31. Alter, *Genesis*, 263.
32. Genesis 44:27 (trans. by Robert Alter, *Genesis*, 264).
33. Alter, *Genesis*, 264.

CHAPTER 4: THE RISE OF WOMEN

1. Mike Dash, "The Woman Who Bested the Men at Math," *Past Imperfect Blog*, August 19, 2011, www.smithsonianmag.com, http://blogs.smithsonianmag.com/history/2011/10/the-woman-who-bested-the-men-at-math/#ixzz2kMvQJWZg.
2. Kay S. Hymowitz, *Manning Up: How the Rise of Women Has Turned Men into Boys* (New York: Basic Books, 2011), 58.
3. Hanna Rosin, *The End of Men: And the Rise of Women* (New York: Riverhead, 2012), 149–50.
4. "Pray the Devil Back to Hell," October 18, 2011, www.pbs.org/wnet/women-war-and-peace/full-episodes/pray-the-devil-back-to-hell/.
5. Tom Brokaw, "Welcome to the Century of Women," April 29, 2013, www.leanin.org, http://leanin.org/discussions/welcome-to-the-century-of-women/.

6. See Judges 4:4–5:7.
7. Tokunboh Adeyemo, gen. ed., "Judges," *Africa Bible Commentary* (Grand Rapids: Zondervan, 2006), 300.
8. John Piper and Wayne Grudem, "An Overview of Central Concerns," in *Recovering Biblical Manhood and Womanhood: A Response to Evangelical Feminism* (Wheaton, IL: Crossway, 1991), 72.
9. Ibid.
10. Thomas R. Schreiner, "The Ministries of Women in the Context of Male Leadership: A Survey of Old and New Testament Examples and Teaching," in *Recovering Biblical Manhood and Womanhood: A Response to Evangelical Feminism*, ed. John Piper and Wayne Grudem (Wheaton, IL: Crossway Books, 1991), 216.
11. Ibid.
12. Ailish Ferguson Eve, "Judges," in *The IVP Women's Bible Commentary*, ed. Catherine Clark Kroeger and Mary J. Evans (Downers Grove, IL: InterVarsity Press, 2002), 133.
13. Ibid., 133–34.
14. Daniel I. Block, *Judges, Ruth,* The New American Commentary (Nashville: Broadman & Holman, 1999), 209–10.
15. Judges 5.
16. Exodus 18:13–26; Judges 4:4–5.
17. Judges 4:17 (NLT).
18. Bruce K. Waltke, *An Old Testament Theology* (Grand Rapids: Zondervan, 2007), 601.
19. Judges 5:24.
20. Hebrews 11:32–34.
21. J. Clinton McCann, *Judges*, Interpretation: A Bible Commentary for Teaching and Preaching (Louisville, KY: Westminster John Knox, 2011), 49.
22. Block, *Judges, Ruth*, 225.
23. Adeyemo, "Judges," 301.
24. Psalm 34:17–18.
25. Judges 4:4.
26. Judges 4:3.
27. "Indeed, one wonders why the narrator would have inserted this parenthetical reference to the settlement of petty civil disputes when the issue in the chapter is a national crisis. This seems to have been the conclusion of the Massoretes, [who translate] … 'for *the* judgment.' This reading suggests a particular issue is in mind, not a series of cases or a routine fulfillment of professional duties. In the present context, the issue that concerns the Israelites is their oppression at the hands of Sisera and the Canaanites" (Block, *Judges, Ruth*, 197).

28. Judges 4:4, 6.

29. Block, *Judges, Ruth*, 199.

30. The NIV translation of Judges 4:9 seems to imply that Deborah is rebuking Barak: " 'Certainly I will go with you,' said Deborah. 'But *because of the course you are taking*, the honor will not be yours, for the Lord will deliver Sisera into the hands of a woman' " (NIV, italics added). The ESV, NASB, NKJV, and NRSV all prefer a translation that simply indicates Barak's mission is being revised: "She said, 'I will surely go with you; nevertheless, the honor shall not be yours *on the journey that you are about to take*, for the Lord will sell Sisera into the hands of a woman.' Then Deborah arose and went with Barak to Kedesh" (NASB, italics added).

31. See Judges 9, especially vv. 52–54.

32. Barry G. Webb, *The Book of Judges*, New International Commentary on the Old Testament (Grand Rapids: Eerdmans, 2012), 181.

33. Judges 5:8b.

34. Luke 14:31–32 (emphasis added).

35. McCann, *Judges*, 52.

36. "Then the fire of the LORD fell and burned up the sacrifice, the wood, the stones and the soil, and also licked up the water in the trench" (1 Kings 18:38).

37. Judges 5.

38. Adeyemo, "Judges," 301.

39. Judges 4:17–18.

40. Block, *Judges, Ruth*, 209.

41. Webb, *The Book of Judges*, 184.

CHAPTER 5: THE POWER OF POWER

1. Boyd, *The Men We Long to Be*, 210.

2. 1 Peter 3:7.

3. Nicki Lisa Cole, "Full Transcript of Emma Watson's Speech on Gender Equality at the UN," http://sociology.about.com/od/Current-Events-in-Sociological-Context/fl/Full-Transcript-of-Emma-Watsons-Speech-on-Gender-Equality-at-the-UN.htm.

4. Rod Norland, "Afghan Mullah Who Raped Girl in His Mosque Receives 20-Year Prison Sentence," *New York Times*, October 24, 2014, 2.

5. Genesis 1:28.

6. Crouch, *Playing God: Redeeming the Gift of Power*, 34–35.

7. Ibid.

8. Cole, "Full Transcript of Emma Watson's Speech on Gender Equality at the UN."

9. Boyd, *The Men We Long to Be*, 88.

10. Despite India's Dowry Prohibition Act of 1961, outlawing dowry in India, the custom is still practiced.

11. For a more thorough treatment of the book of Ruth, see James, *The Gospel of Ruth*.

12. Ruth 1:13.

13. Isaiah 10:1–2 (emphasis added).

14. R. Laird Harris, Gleason L. Archer Jr., Bruce K. Waltke, eds., *Theological Word Book of the Old Testament* (Chicago: Moody Bible Institute, 1980), 1:271–72.

15. Ruth 1:11, 12, 13; 2:2, 8, 22; and 3:1, 10, 11, 16, 18.

16. James, *The Gospel of Ruth*, 140.

17. Matthew 13:45–46.

18. "When you reap the harvest of your land, do not reap to the very edges of your field or gather the gleanings of your harvest. Do not go over your vineyard a second time or pick up the grapes that have fallen. Leave them for the poor and the foreigner. I am the LORD your God" (Leviticus 19:9–10, TNIV).

   "When you are harvesting your crops and forget to bring in a bundle of grain from your field, don't go back to get it. Leave it for the foreigners, orphans, and widows. Then the LORD your God will bless you in all you do. When you beat the olives from your olive trees, don't go over the boughs twice. Leave some of the olives for the foreigners, orphans, and widows. When you gather the grapes in your vineyard, don't glean the vines after they are picked. Leave the remaining grapes for the foreigners, orphans, and widows. Remember that you were slaves in the land of Egypt. That is why I am giving you this command" (Deuteronomy 24:19–22, NLT).

19. "If brothers are living together and one of them dies without a son, his widow must not marry outside the family. Her husband's brother shall take her and marry her and fulfill the duty of a brother-in-law to her. The first son she bears shall carry on the name of the dead brother so that his name will not be blotted out from Israel. However, if a man does not want to marry his brother's wife, she shall go to the elders at the town gate and say, 'My husband's brother refuses to carry on his brother's name in Israel. He will not fulfill the duty of a brother-in-law to me.' Then the elders of his town shall summon him and talk to him. If he persists in saying, 'I do not want to marry her,' his brother's widow shall go up to him in the presence of the elders, take off one of his sandals, spit in his face and say, 'This is what is done to the man who will not build up his brother's family line'" (Deuteronomy 25:5–9).

20. "But Naomi said, 'Return home, my daughters. Why would you come

with me? Am I going to have any more sons, who could become your husbands? Return home, my daughters; I am too old to have another husband. Even if I thought there was still hope for me—even if I had a husband tonight and then gave birth to sons—would you wait until they grew up? Would you remain unmarried for them? No, my daughters. It is more bitter for me than for you, because the Lord's hand has turned against me!' " (Ruth 1:11–13, TNIV).

21. Ruth 1:11–12.
22. "If one of your fellow Israelites becomes poor and sells some of their property, their nearest relative is to come and redeem what they have sold" (Leviticus 25:25).
23. Ruth's country of origin is today's Jordan and a founding member of the Arab League. According to today's demographics, Ruth would be classified as an Arab.
24. It would be the height of cruelty and selfishness for Naomi to send her barren daughter-in-law on a mission to bear a child, and Naomi doesn't. She is seeking safety for Ruth who Naomi expects will outlive her. Based on Boaz's kindnesses throughout the harvest season, he seems the most likely of all the men in Bethlehem, to be willing to accept such a proposal. Ruth, however, isn't about to abandon Naomi and begin seeking a husband for herself. She is still battling for Naomi, and more specifically intent on rescuing Elimelech from extinction.
25. Ruth 4:6.
26. Ruth 4:13.
27. Crouch, *Playing God: Redeeming the Gift of Power*, 41.
28. Ruth 4:17.

Chapter 6: The Marginalized Man

1. Joseph Pleck, "Understanding Patriarchy and Men's Power," www .nomas.org/node/176.
2. Wesley Yang, "Paper Tigers: What happens to all the Asian-American overachievers when the test-taking ends?" *New York Magazine*, May 8, 2011, http://nymag.com/news/features/asian-americans-2011-5/.
3. Ibid.
4. Sharad Yadav, "Finding the Father," in *Father Factor: American Christian Men on Fatherhood and Faith*, ed. R. Anderson Campbell (Ashland, OR: White Cloud, 2014), 32.
5. Ted Conover, "The Dispossessed: A lawyer personalizes the struggle against injustice with the story of a man wrongfully convicted of murder" (*New York Times Book Review* of Bryan Stevenson's book, *Just Mercy: A Story of Justice and Redemption* [October 19, 2014], 11).

6. "Report of The Sentencing Project to the United Nations Human Rights Committee Regarding Racial Disparities in the United States Criminal Justice System," August 1, 2013. The Sentencing Project is a Washington, D.C., based group that advocates for prison reform.

7. N. T. Wright, *How God Became King: The Forgotten Story of the Gospels* (New York: HarperOne, 2012), 69.

8. Matthew 9:11.

9. Luke 19:2.

10. http://www.allaboutjesuschrist.org/tax-collector-faq.htm.

11. Matthew 14:1.

12. Grant R. Osborne, *Matthew*, Zondervan Exegetical Commentary on the New Testament, ed. Clinton E. Arnold (Grand Rapids: Zondervan, 2010), 334–35.

13. Luke 5:28.

14. Matthew 10:3.

15. Mark 2:15; Luke 5:27, 29.

16. Mark 3:18; Luke 6:14–15; Acts 1:13.

17. Matthew 4:17 (TNIV).

18. Matthew 21:31.

19. Matthew 13:45–46.

20. Matthew 6:21.

21. Matthew 11:28.

22. Matthew 7:7.

23. Matthew 19:24.

24. Osborne, *Matthew*, 720.

25. Matthew 9:10–12; Mark 2:15–17; Luke 5:29–32.

26. Matthew 11:19.

27. James D. G. Dunn and Alan M. Suggate, *The Justice of God: A Fresh Look at the Old Doctrine of Justification by Faith* (Grand Rapids: Eerdmans, 1993), 23.

28. Matthew 9:13; Hosea 6:6.

29. Carolyn Custis James, "The Power of *Hesed*," in *The Gospel of Ruth*, 109–24.

30. Sally Lloyd-Jones, *The Jesus Storybook Bible: Every Story Whispers His Name* (Grand Rapids: Zondervan, 2007), 36.

31. Douglas R. A. Hare, *Matthew*, Interpretation: A Bible Commentary for Teaching and Preaching (Louisville, KY: Westminster John Knox, 1993), 7.

32. W. F. Albright and C. S. Mann, *Matthew*, Anchor Bible (Garden City, NY: Doubleday, 1971), 2.

33. Hare, *Matthew*, 7.

34. N. T. Wright, *Simply Jesus: A New Vision of Who He Was, What He Did, and Why He Matters* (New York: HarperOne, 2011), 218.

CHAPTER 7: GENDER ROLE REVERSAL

1. Shirley Leung, "A Welcome Role Reversal," *The Boston Globe,* June 13, 2014, www.bostonglobe.com/business/2014/06/12/number-stay -home-dads-rising/OnmubpLSzZgC5XLzaO93uM/story.html.
2. Ibid.
3. Gretchen Livingston, "Growing Number of Dads Home with the Kids—Biggest increase among those caring for family," June 5, 2014, Pew Research and Social Demographic Trends, www.pewsocialtrends .org/2014/06/05/growing-number-of-dads-home-with-the-kids/.
4. Leung, "A Welcome Role Reversal."
5. Livingston, "Growing Number of Dads at Home with the Kids."
6. Ibid.
7. Richard H. Thaler, "Breadwinning Wives and Nervous Husbands," *New York Times,* June 1, 2013, www.nytimes.com/2013/06/02/business /breadwinner-wives-and-nervous-husbands.html?pagewanted=all& _r=0.
8. Jessica Bennett, "The Brotherhood of the Stay-at-Home Dad," *New York Times,* November 14, 2014, www.nytimes.com/2014/11/16 /fashion/the-brotherhood-of-the-stay-at-home-dad.html?_r=0.
9. "Jesus was in the eye of the Jewish Law the legitimate descendent of Joseph. For although He had no earthly father, Joseph was nevertheless married to his mother and this established the legal relationship" (Norval Geldenhuys, *Luke,* ed. F. F. Bruce, New International Commentary on the New Testament [Grand Rapids: Eerdmans, 1971], 152).
10. Matthew 1:20b.
11. Matthew 1:20–21; 2:13, 19–20, 22–23.
12. Matthew 5:20.
13. Matthew 1:19.
14. Deuteronomy 22:23–24.
15. Hare, *Matthew,* 9.
16. W. F. Albright and C. S. Mann, *Matthew,* Anchor Bible (Garden City, NY: Doubleday, 1971), 8.
17. Wright, *Simply Jesus,* 218.
18. Jeremiah 9:23–24 (NLT, emphasis added).
19. Matthew 3:17.
20. Beth Stebner, "The last faces of American slavery: Stunning pictures of men and women who were born into slavery and photographed more than 70 years after being freed," *DailyMail Online,* April 1, 2012, www.dailymail.co.uk/news/article-2123695/Steal-away-home -Stunning-portraits-men-women-born-slavery-photographed-seventy -years-Emancipation-Proclamation.html#ixzz3IsAPpLre.
21. Dunn and Suggate, *The Justice of God,* 33.

22. Mark 12:28.
23. Mark 12:30–31.
24. James, *Half the Church*, 146.
25. Luke 1:38 (NASB).
26. For further reading, see Kenneth E. Bailey, *Jesus Through Middle Eastern Eyes: Cultural Studies in the Gospels* (Carol Stream, IL: InterVarsity Press, 2008), and Verlyn D. Verbrugge, *A Not-So-Silent Night: The Unheard Story of Christmas and Why It Matters* (Grand Rapids: Kregel, 2009).
27. Matthew 2:2.
28. Luke 2:46–47.
29. Luke 2:48–49.
30. Matthew 1:19.

CHAPTER 8: THE MANHOOD OF JESUS

1. R. T. France, *Jesus the Radical* (Leicester, UK: Inter-Varsity Press, 1989), 13.
2. John 13:23.
3. John 21:25 (NLT).
4. Wright, *How God Became King*, 11.
5. See Carolyn Custis James, "Here Comes the Bride!" *Half the Church*, 119–34.
6. Stanley Grenz, "Biblical Priesthood and Women in Ministry," *Discovering Biblical Equality: Complementarity without Hierarchy*, ed. Ronald W. Pierce and Rebecca Merrill Groothuis (Downers Grove, IL: InterVarsity Press, 2004), 282.
7. Ibid.
8. Walter Brueggemann, *The Prophetic Imagination* (Minneapolis: Fortress, 2001), 86.
9. Albert H. Newman, *Nicene and Post-Nicene Fathers*, vol. 4, series 1, *St. Augustine, Writings Against the Manicheans and Against the Donatists*, ed. Philip Schaff (Grand Rapids: Eerdmans, 2005), 29.
10. Isaiah 53:2.
11. This data comes from a 2001 study sponsored by the BBC, France 3, and the Discovery Channel, in which forensic anthropologist Richard Neave of the University of Manchester, constructed the face of what Jesus might have looked like based on a first-century Jewish skull.
12. This is influenced by what the apostle Paul writes regarding first-century standards: "if a man has long hair it is a disgrace to him" (1 Corinthians 11:14).
13. Scot McKnight, *The King Jesus Gospel: The Original Good News Revisited* (Grand Rapids: Zondervan, 2011), 138.

14. Luke 2:49.
15. Mark Binelli, "Pope Francis: The Times They Are A-Changin'," *Rolling Stone Magazine,* January 28, 2014, www.rollingstone .com/culture/news/pope-francis-the-times-they-are-a-changin -20140128#ixzz3KaDkAxmE.
16. John 18:36.
17. John 1:1.
18. John 1:18.
19. Hebrews 1:3.
20. Philippians 2:6 (NIV text note). The ESV, NASB, and NKJV also translate "in the form of God."
21. John 14:7–9.
22. John 8:28–29.
23. Matthew 6:9–13.
24. John 8:49, 55.
25. Wright, *How God Became King,* 47.
26. Donald A. Hagner, *Matthew 1-13,* Word Biblical Commentary, ed. David A. Hubbard and Glenn W. Barker (Dallas: Word, 1993), 70.
27. Rohr, *From Wild Man to Wise Man,* 16.
28. Matthew 20:20–28, esp. 26–27.
29. John 13:15.
30. Matthew 14:15–16 (emphasis added).
31. Matthew 19:13–14.
32. Mark 10:46–52.
33. Matthew 15:21–28.
34. John 11:32–35; Luke 19:41.
35. Galatians 5:22–23.
36. Luke 8:1–4.
37. Luke 10:38–42.
38. John 11:1–46.
39. Matthew 26:6–13; John 12:1–8.
40. Matthew 16:22.
41. Matthew 26:10–13.
42. Grenz, "Biblical Priesthood and Women in Ministry," 282.

CHAPTER 9: LIBERATING MEN FROM THE MALESTROM

1. Frank A. James III and John D. Woodbridge, *Church History,* vol. 2: *From Pre-Reformation to the Present Day* (Grand Rapids: Zondervan, 2013), 721.
2. Ibid., 722.
3. Ibid.

4. Alexander Smith, "Nigeria's Boko Haram Violence Now Comparable to ISIS in Iraq," NBCNews, www.nbcnews.com/storyline/missing-nigeria-schoolgirls/nigerias-boko-haram-violence-now-comparable-isis-iraq-n260576.

5. Drew G. I. Hart, "We aren't playing the race card; we are analyzing the racialized deck," *Christian Century,* December 8, 2014, www.christiancentury.org/blogs/archive/2014-12/we-are-t-playing-race-card-we-are-analyzing-racialized-deck#.VIYAHEhoB_A.google_pluseone_share.

6. Ibid.,

7. Acts 9:1.

8. Dunn and Suggate, *The Justice of God,* 22.

9. Philippians 3:6.

10. Dunn and Suggate, *The Justice of God,* 23.

11. Ibid.

12. Ibid.

13. Acts 8:1–3.

14. Acts 9:3–5.

15. Acts 9:26.

16. James and Woodbridge, *Church History,* vol. 2, 722.

17. Ibid.

18. 1 Timothy 1:12–17.

19. Acts 23:6.

20. Acts 9:15.

21. Acts 16:11–15, 40.

22. Philippians 4:2–3.

23. Romans 16:1–2.

24. Romans 16:3.

25. Romans 16:7.

26. Romans 16:12.

27. Romans 16:13.

28. Philemon 12.

29. Philemon 16.

30. Ibid.

31. Galatians 3:28 (TNIV).

32. Philippians 2:12.

33. John 8:32.